Victim Compensation

Victim Compensation

Economic, Legal, and Political Aspects

Roger E. Meiners
Law and Economics Center
University of Miami School of Law

Lexington Books
D.C. Heath and Company
Lexington, Massachusetts
Toronto

Library of Congress Cataloging in Publication Data

Meiners, Roger E.
Victim compensation.

A revision of the author's thesis, Virginia Polytechnic Institute.
Bibliography: p.
Includes index.
1. Reparation. 2. Victims of crimes. I. Title.
HV8688.M44   1978   362.8'8   77-80772
ISBN 0-669-01667-5

Published simultaneously in Canada

Printed in the United States of America

International Standard Book Number: 0-669-01667-5

Library of Congress Catalog Card Number: 77-80772

To Chris

Contents

List of Figures

List of Tables

Foreword

Although proposals for victim compensation can be traced back nearly four thousand years, their implementation is a relatively recent phenomenon. At present, approximately one-half of the states have introduced or adopted some form of state assistance to victims of crimes (including Montana and Oregon since this study was completed). In addition, the House of Representatives has passed its first bill endorsing the concept of federal grants to states that provide assistance to individuals hurt by criminals. The congressional bill of September 1977 differs from the bill passed previously by the Senate. It is expected that the differences may be resolved in 1978 when the Senate again considers the legislation.

In this book, Professor Roger E. Meiners surveys the development of victim-compensation schemes in the United States and in other countries. He also offers the first comprehensive legal and economic analysis of the incentives facing politicians, administrative officials, criminals, and their victims. The breadth and depth of this study should appeal to a wide audience.

Those interested in the historical development of the victim-compensation principle and the associated debate will find a comprehensive survey in chapter two. This chapter also investigates various victim-compensation schemes in New Zealand, Great Britain, Northern Ireland, Australia, Canada, and other nations. In chapter three, various American state-compensation schemes are described, ranging from direct payments to victims of crime in Maryland to restitution by the criminal in Georgia.

More important, the author examines the incentive structures of victims, politicians, and criminals as they would evolve under a typical compensation scheme such as that proposed by the current Congress. The resulting consequences are critically examined by using the tools of economic analysis in the context of the particular legal arrangements for victim compensation, an approach that exemplifies the unique combination of law and economic analysis. In a public-choice framework, chapter four concentrates on the potential costs, political pressures, and incentives of politicians implementing compensation as well as those who would administer the program. The equity issues surrounding compensation are discussed in chapter five.

In chapters six and seven, Professor Meiners analyzes the possible responses of criminals and of potential victims to typical compensation schemes. Various moral-hazard and deterrence responses by both criminals and victims receive special attention in these chapters.

The study is unique in several respects. It is the first study that attempts to answer the fundamental questions surrounding victim compensation: To what extent do the states have a duty to compensate citizens for harm from criminal actions? Are existing civil remedies adequate? To what extent would victim

compensation replace private individual insurance? Would national health care serve as an alternative to the proposed victim-compensation programs? How do victim-compensation schemes affect the incentives and behavior of criminals and potential victims?

In answering these questions, Professor Meiners reminds us that the principles of justice and fairness that arise in determining alternatives for helping unfortunate members of society are plagued by various economic and political realities. Thus, most methods of victim compensation imply that potential victims would spend fewer resources and less effort in avoiding hazardous situations. Although not easily detectable, contributory negligence by potential victims is likely to increase. Equally important, legislators, administrators, and other parties involved in the provision of funds to compensate victims will respond to the invisible hand of self-interest in the design and execution of programs originally intended to help only those who meet unfortunate outcomes outside their control. His analysis also reminds us that the deterrence effects for reducing criminal actions may be greatly weakened under a scheme of victim compensation.

A careful reading of the book reveals one overriding conclusion: more careful study of existing civil remedies, private insurance, and state victim compensation and restitution experiences is clearly in order. These studies may never be fulfilled if a federal program forces the direction of the individual efforts currently proposed and executed among the individual states.

Kenneth W. Clarkson

Law and Economics Center
University of Miami School of Law
October 1977

Preface

The idea of governmental compensation for the victims of crime first came to my attention about five years ago. At first, like many ideas, the effects of victim compensation appeared to be straightforward and to promote equitable outcomes. Several nonobvious consequences of victim compensation were pointed out to me by Professor Gordon Tullock at the Center for Study of Public Choice at Virginia Polytechnic Institute. Professor Tullock's initial criticism was responsible for forcing me to think more carefully about this topic, which eventually became my doctoral dissertation at Virginia Polytechnic Institute. A number of others at VPI, especially Professor Richard Wagner, my committee chairman, and Professors James M. Buchanan, M.M. Ott, and W. Mark Crain, were helpful in my research.

The present version of this research has been greatly modified by my postdoctoral legal and economic training at the Law and Economics Center of the University of Miami School of Law. A number of individuals at the Law and Economics Center, especially Kenneth W. Clarkson, Louis De Alessi, and James S. Mofsky, have helped me in thinking about this topic. The John M. Olin Foundation is due thanks for financial support during my stay at the Law and Economics Center.

Roger E. Meiners

John M. Olin Fellow
Law and Economics Center
Coral Gables, Florida

1 Introduction

". . . Under several systems in early American law, a thief, in addition to his punishment, was ordered to return three times the value of the stolen goods, or in case of insolvency to place his person at the disposal of the victim for a certain time."[1] Today only a minute percentage of the victims of criminal attacks receive any payment from the person who committed the act.

In the past decade there has been increasing interest in the financial losses suffered by the victims of crime. This concern has been manifested in legislation that would enable some victims of criminal acts to collect a payment from the state for the money value of the losses they have suffered in attacks. This procedure is generally called victim compensation.

Definitional Limitations

Because "victim" is a broader concept than "crime," it is necessary to distinguish victims of natural forces, accidents, and civil wrongs from the victims of criminal acts. Only actions made criminal by the law and of serious consequence to the victims, such as murder, rape, robbery, and arson, are under consideration.[2] The death or injury must be sustained by an "innocent" victim. Usually this means that the degree of contributory negligence by the victims will emerge as a test of victimization. When the victim is found to have consented to the act, or incited the criminal to act, he is not likely to be judged an innocent victim. However, exposing oneself to high-risk situations is generally not considered contributory negligence.[3]

In the modern context, compensation is generally meant to be the "granting of public funds to persons who have been victimized by a crime of violence and to persons who survive those killed by such crime. . . ."[4] These payments are usually for medical costs and loss of wages incurred by the victim, and possibly compensation for pain and suffering, but generally not for the value of property lost except for items lost in an attack on the person. Often there is to be no connection between the criminal and the victim in this process, unlike the situation in most compensation schemes throughout history.

Scope of This Study

There are numerous issues surrounding victim compensation, some of which do not readily appear to be related to the topic, at least as it has been typically

1

discussed. The traditional issues will be considered in this chapter. This topic arouses many questions that are relevant to the analysis of other public programs. Currently most costs of victimization are borne by the private sector. Victim compensation would require the public sector to absorb many of these costs. Since some crime insurance would be moved from the private to the public sector, it is important to study the desirability of such a change in liability.

The plight of the victim has become a greater social, political, and economic problem, due to the growth of crime. The impact that public compensation would have on the status of all potential crime victims needs to be studied. The sheer magnitude of the costs that crime imposes on society underscores the need for economic analysis of the criminal-victim relationship. Crime may well account for ten percent of the gross national product. One estimate, the validity of which is not clear, is that "white collar" crimes alone cost about $40 billion a year.[5]

The methodology of public choice is aptly suited for analytical application to governmental compensation programs. This analysis will suggest, in a positive framework, what can be expected to emerge in operation if the present federal proposal for victim compensation is adopted. Such an analysis will take account of the motives of the participants involved, the origins of the program, its political support, and the likely manner of operation. The theory of bureaucracy is especially applicable in this instance; moreover, the enactment of victim compensation will even provide a test of the predictive abilities of this theory.

Equity considerations need to be developed in considering the role of the victim in the framework of a democratic society. Most equity considerations are tied to emotional pleas and political norms of justice. Employing a Rawlsian framework for examining such equity issues as justice and fairness for victims may help to avoid one of the traditional pitfalls of equity discussions.

As a proposed public program that may involve substantial sums of money, victim compensation also raises important issues concerning efficiency. The impact of the proposed program on victims and criminals can be considered, as can the specific organization of the proposed program. The system can be compared to alternatives, such as other forms of public programs, or simply compared to the private insurance system that operates currently. These and other issues will be developed in this study.

Traditional Rationales for Victim Compensation

To this point the discussion of victim compensation has been carried on almost exclusively by members of the legal profession. The rationales for compensation by the state can be found in many of the scores of articles written on the topic in the last decade. The major arguments can be summarized as follows: the duty of the state to protect citizens, the inadequacy of civil remedies for crime victims, the inequities of the income distribution, and the sociological view that crime is the fault of society in general.

The argument made by many proponents of state compensation for victims is that "the state has a duty to protect its citizens from crime and that if it fails to do so it incurs an obligation to indemnify those who are victimized."[6] This is the primary argument used in advocating the federal proposal for compensation by former Senator Mike Mansfield, joint author of the Mansfield-McClellan compromise version of the Victims of Crime Act, who said, "If society fails in its efforts to provide basic protection, then the social contract has been breached; the citizen has suffered."[7]

This argument must be made on normative grounds in Western jurisdictions. In the strict sense the argument is legally groundless. One lawyer who favors compensation notes that "it is doubtful . . . that any underlying liability of the state for the criminal acts of third parties actually exists."[8]

Compensation is technically more of a welfare payment than an insurance payment. As the writers of the 1964 British compensation program noted:

Compensation will be paid *ex gratia*. The government does not accept that the state is liable for injuries caused to people by the acts of others. The public does, however, feel a sense of responsibility for . . . the innocent victim, and it is right that his feeling should find practical expression in the provision of compensation. . . . [9]

Indeed, with the possible exceptions of New Zealand and Northern Ireland, none of the jurisdictions establishing crime-compensation programs has accepted the theory that the government has a duty to compensate victims.[10]

One strange aspect about the argument of proponents of state liability for criminal costs is that it specifically limits compensation to personal injury. "This limitation is neither inherent, nor natural, and, in addition, seems to possess a great number of crimino-political disadvantages." The argument should apply "with equal vigor to harm property, or honor, etc.," in order to be consistent.[11] This limitation has been noticed recently, and there are numerous proposals to expand the coverage of victim compensation. This expansion is to be expected, as will be demonstrated later when the impact of the bureaucracy on compensation is considered, so that the concern that a public-compensation program may be inadequate in coverage is probably only a short-run problem for proponents.

Another argument made in favor of public payments to victims is based on the inadequacy of civil action against criminals. A victim of criminal attack may, in some jurisdictions, and for some crimes, bring civil action against his assailant for all pecuniary and nonpecuniary losses. This is of little practicable use to victims, as the majority of criminal assailants are not apprehended or even identifiable by the victims.[12] Of those who are apprehended, few are of legal age to be subject to such action or have the resources to pay for the costs of the damages they have inflicted. For instance, it has been estimated that 90 percent or more of the inmates of the federal prison in Atlanta are indigent, in that they could not raise as much as $300 to retain legal counsel.[13]

A study of 167 victims of violént crimes in Toronto in 1966 disclosed that although 75 percent of the victims incurred pecuniary losses, only 15 percent considered suing for reparation, only 5.4 percent consulted a lawyer, and only 4.8 percent actually did try to collect from their attackers. Only three of the 167, or 1.8 percent of the victims, actually did collect anything from their attackers.[14]

The argument that civil action is inadequate in providing relief to victims is well taken but is rarely accompanied by an analysis of the law that has made civil suit against criminal assailants so rare. While it is certain that, due to the low rate of criminal capture, a civil suit would be effective in only a small minority of cases of criminal attack, such suits would be more common were it not for the distinction in Anglo-Saxon law between civil and criminal cases.

Civil relief is impaired because, in general,

a criminal judgment of conviction or acquittal is not admissible in a civil action, even as evidence of the facts. . . . The victim's time and testimony in the criminal action must be repeated and the additional cost of proving the offense before a civil jury is on him.[15]

This separation of civil and criminal law is often surprising and confusing to laymen. Whether sensible or not, as common law developed, especially in the last four centuries, there has been a greater and greater legal distance placed between the criminal and his victim.

A criminal act is an offense against the state, while a tort is an offense against the individual. Hence, if a man is captured and found guilty of rape, he is punished by the state because rape injured society. His victim may sue him, but not for rape, since that was a criminal act. She must sue in tort for civil damages such as medical expenses, loss of income, pain and suffering, etc., but this requires that the victim bear the expense in civil court of proving the act of rape.

This weakening of the potential for victims to receive restitution from criminals developed over a long period of time. Since the civil-criminal distinction has worsened the position of the victim, it would seem more logical to change the law and its attendant weaknesses rather than to paper over the process with public payments. In any event, it is not necessarily a logical conclusion that inadequate civil remedies should be replaced by public compensation since private compensation is available. As of 1973 almost 94 percent of the population in the United States had insurance to cover surgical expenses, 84 percent had insurance for regular medical expenses, and 78 percent had insurance for major medical expenses.[16]

Another argument raised in favor of compensation pertains to considerations of income equality. It has been claimed that low income may preclude the purchase of insurance. Another perceived problem with the regime of private insurance is that "the victim will have to bear the cost, at least of the premium payments, to protect himself from the antisocial, criminal activities of

another."[17] Rather, this particular author argues, society should bear the cost of compensating the victim.

Some proponents, such as the one just cited, appear to believe that if society provides victim compensation then victims will not have to bear the costs of private insurance. The notion that services provided by the government are free generally has been recognized as false even by the most staunch supporters of massive public-welfare programs. Public compensation would operate something like private insurance; taxes paid to the government would substitute for private insurance premiums. The real concern here is that some crime victims are in financial need because they did not have sufficient private insurance or savings to cover the losses they suffered.

The argument that society should help some victims because they are in financial need is a purely normative judgment. Most legislative bodies that have established compensation programs have stated that the rationale was humanitarian and was not based on the liability of the state for these expenses. The role of economic theory here is to point out the costs and benefits of such a program, so that normative judgments can be made in light of positive analysis. However, this study will also consider, in a more rigorous framework than is commonly employed, the equity arguments that apply to this situation.

The last major argument made in favor of public payments to victims is based on a normative sociological position. Compensation is viewed as desirable due to "the responsibility which society must bear for the crime itself. Crime is, after all, a sociological and economic problem as well as a problem of individual criminality."[18] Some sociologists argue that there is a general societal responsibility for violent behavior because violence is the product of acculturation of the young into patterns of violence, and is also due to the exclusion of some groups from normal political participation.[19]

The sociological argument that society has caused people to commit criminal acts, and therefore society should pay the victim, is debatable on scientific grounds. The economic view of man as responsive to incentives to commit crime and to punishment received for crime committed does not square with the sociological argument advanced by some scholars. In general, the weight of empirical evidence at the present time would support the punishment of criminals over alternative actions as the most effective deterrent to crime.[20] This evidence tends to refute the sociological view of criminal activity.

The basic justifications for victim compensation, as they presently exist and are generally proposed, must rest on normative humanitarian grounds, since the legal arguments have little weight and the sociological argument is subject to severe dispute. This is not to say, of course, that compensation programs of a different form and/or under different systems of legal organization may not be defensible on other than humanitarian grounds. This book is designed to present some new arguments about public compensation, based on positive methodology, in order to allow normative decisions in an informed setting.

Notes

1. E. Ruggles-Brise, *Report to the Secretary of State for the Home Department on the Proceedings of the Fifth and Sixth International Penitentiary Congresses* (London, 1901), pp. 51-52, quoted in Stephen Schafer, *The Victim and His Criminal* (New York: Random House, 1968), p. 14.

2. LeRoy L. Lamborn, "Toward a Victim Orientation in Criminal Theory," *Rutgers Law Review* 22 (1968), pp. 736-38.

3. Richard Cosway, "Crime Compensation," *Washington Law Review* 49 (1974), pp. 561-62.

4. Herbert Edelhertz and Gilbert Geis, *Public Compensation to Victims of Crime* (New York: Praeger Publishers, Inc., 1974), p. 3.

5. U.S., National Institute of Law Enforcement and Criminal Justice, *Exemplary Projects: Prosecution of Economic Crimes* (Washington, D.C.: U.S.G.P.O., 1975), p. 1.

6. Bruce R. Jacob, Reparation or Restitution by the Criminal Offender to His Victim," *Journal of Criminal Law, Criminology and Police Science* 61 (1970), p. 153.

7. Mike Mansfield, "Justice for Victims of Crime," *Houston Law Review* 9 (September 1971), p. 77.

8. Cosway, "Crime Compensation," p. 553.

9. Great Britain, Home Office and Scottish Home and Health Department, *Compensation for Victims of Crime and Violence*, Cmnd. 2323 Para. 8 (1964), quoted from Cosway, "Crime Compensation," p. 463.

10. LeRoy L. Lamborn, "Propriety of Governmental Compensation of Victims of Crime." *George Washington Law Review* 41 (March 1973), p. 463.

11. G.O.W. Mueller, "Compensation for Victims of Crime: Thought before Action," *Minnesota Law Review* 50 (December 1965), pp. 214, 217.

12. Lamborn, "Propriety of Governmental Compensation," p. 452.

13. Jacob, "Reparation or Restitution," p. 152.

14. Allen M. Linden, "Victims of Crime and Tort Law." *Canadian Bar Journal* 12 (February 1969), p. 21.

15. Joan M. Covey, "Alternatives to a Compensation Plan for Victims of Physical Violence," *Dickinson Law Review* 69 (Summer 1965), p. 398.

16. Health Insurance Institute, *Source Book of Health Insurance Data 1974-75* (New York:Health Insurance Institute, 16th ed.), p. 27.

17. Boyd L. Wright, "What About the Victims?" *North Dakota Law Review* 48 (Spring 1972), p. 479.

18. Arthur J. Goldberg. "Preface" (Symposium on victim compensation) *Southern California Law Review* 43 (1970), pp. 1-2.

19. Marvin E. Wolfgang, "Social Responsibility for Violent Behavior," *Southern California Law Review* 43 (1970), p. 6.

20. See Gordon Tullock, "Does Punishment Deter Crime?" *Public Interest* 36 (1974); Isaac Ehrlich, "The Deterrent Effect of Capital Punishment: A Question of Life and Death," *American Economic Review* 65 (June 1975).

2 Historical and Foreign Methods of Compensation

The History of Victim Compensation

The Babylonian Code of Hammurabi, more than four thousand years old, is often cited as the first legal record of victim compensation. In part it reads:

If the brigand has not been taken, the man plundered shall claim before God what he has lost; and the city and sheriff in whose land and boundary the theft has taken place shall restore to him all that he has lost. If a life, the city and sheriff shall pay one mina of silver to his people.[1]

Such compensation was, however, the exception rather than the rule in the Code of Hammurabi and in most other ancient codes. The primary focus of ancient law was on restitution from the criminal to the victim, not on compensation from the state to the victim. It has been suggested that in the few instances of compensation in history, it was "motivated less by a concern for the victim than by a desire to punish society for failing to find the criminal."[2]

According to Sir Henry Maine, author of one of the most scholarly works on the development of law, "the penal Law of ancient communities is not the law of Crimes; it is the law of. . .Torts. The person injured proceeds against the wrong-doer by an ordinary civil action, and recovers . . .money-damages if he succeeds."[3] Hence, many offenses which we view as crimes were treated exclusively as torts under Roman law. These torts included theft, assault, violent robbery, trespass, libel, and slander. "All alike gave rise to an obligation. . .and were all requited by a payment of money."[4] Similarly, the "Laws of the Germanic tribes" all describe a system of restitution payments from homicide on down.[5] Under Anglo-Saxon law a sum was placed on every injury that could be done to one's person, civil rights, honor, or peace.

Since citizens depended upon the law of tort, and not upon a law of crime, for protection, then the person who suffered the wrong, not the state, was conceived to have been wronged. While there were laws punishing acts against the state, and torts, in general, unlike today, there was little notion of "injury to the community."[6] This was most notable, according to Sir Henry Maine, by the fact that at trial "the magistrate carefully simulated the demeanour of a private arbitrator casually called in."[7] In the early European courts (Roman, Greek, Germanic, and Anglo-Saxon) the state did not take money from the defendant for any wrong done to the state, but claimed a share in the restitution "awarded to the plaintiff as the fair price of its time and trouble."[8]

7

An example of the detailed payments to be made for various offenses is illustrated by the Dooms of King Alfred of the ninth century:

A man who "lay with a maiden belonging to the king" had to pay 50 shillings, but if she were a "grindling slave" the compensation was halved. Compensation for lying with a nobleman's serving maid was assessed still lower at 12 shillings.[9]

Penalties such as death were prescribed by the courts not as punishment by the state, but in lieu of the vengeance the victim wished to inflict upon the criminal. The court acted as a middleman in an effort to establish order.

Criminal jurisprudence developed when "the State conceived itself to be wronged, and the Popular Assembly struck straight at the offender. . . ."[10] The notion of "sins" which were to be punished by an authority was not original with Christians, but did help to develop the dichotomy between civil and criminal law. Sir Henry Maine reports that the Church, in an attempt to bring order and to gain authority, found a basis in Scripture for the power of punishment by the civil authorities. "There can be no doubt. . .that modern ideas on the subject of crime are based upon two assumptions contended for by the Church in the Dark Ages. . ." that the state was the representative of the Church with respect to crime, and that the Church was capable of defining crimes.[11]

The origins of the passage of payments from the criminal to the state instead of to the victim was explained by King Alfred:

They [Church authorities] then ordained that, out of that mercy which Christ had taught, secular lords, with their leave, might without sin take for every misdeed the *bot* in money which they ordained; except in cases of treason against a lord, to which they dared not assign any mercy because Almighty God adjudged none to them that despise Him, nor did Christ adjudge any to them which sold Him to death; and he commanded that a lord be loved like Himself.[12]

The growth of royal and ecclesiastical authority in the Middle Ages contributed to a sharpening division between tort law and criminal law. By the twelfth century the victim's right to reparation was largely replaced by fines assessed by a state tribunal against the offender. More offenses came to be considered crimes against society, or breaking the "king's peace," so that punishment was to be meted out by the king, and the king would be compensated.[13] The development of common law eliminated most restitution as civil and criminal law became more distinct with the passage of time.

A few vestiges of restitution remained, such as in seventeenth-century colonial American law. According to limited court records from the 1670s restitution was imposed on criminals in about one-half of the theft cases in some Massachusetts counties. It was also imposed in cases of manslaughter, assault and battery, burglary, and lewd, lascivious, and wanton behavior.[14] It was common for a thief to be "required to make restitution, sometimes

threefold, sometimes double. The law left the matter largely to the judge but provided specifically for treble restitution for stealing from a person's yard or 'orchid.'" Servants who could not meet the payment would have their term of service extended and a "completely destitute thief faced the possibility of being sold into slavery, for the Bible has set the precedent for dealing with this type: 'if he have nothing, then he shall be sold for theft.' "[15]

The revival of restitution and compensation was considered during the nineteenth-century movement for penal change. Jeremy Bentham advocated the return of compensation, holding that " 'satisfaction' should be drawn from the offender's property, but 'if the offender is without property. . .it ought to be furnished out of the public treasury, because it is an object of public good. . . .' "[16] The restitution of crime victims was also discussed at each of the five International Prison Congresses held during the latter part of that century. Almost all eminent criminologists hailed various forms of restitution as desirable, generally in the form of direct payment from the criminal to his victim, either immediately or through prison wages. Garofalo noted that "a fund of this sort existed in the Kingdom of the Two Sicilies as well as in the Duchy of Tuscany, but it never appears to have been of much service to claimants, as the treasury always put it under contribution to defray the expenses of the courts."[17]

Modern Revival of Compensation

Serious discussion of victim compensation was revived in England in the early 1950s. Many credit the writings of Margaret Fry, a British advocate of penal change, as influential in bringing the topic to public attention.[18] Fry originally proposed, in the vein of the historical form of compensation, that the criminal make reparation to his victim as a part of the rehabilitation process. However, Fry soon decided that the historical form of compensation was impractical, and in the late 1950s advocated state responsibility for victims' injuries.[19] According to the common view of the recent legal history of compensation, Fry was so influential that her work led to the adoption of compensation in Great Britain, New Zealand, and several other jurisdictions around the world.

Compensation in New Zealand. New Zealand was the first Anglo-Saxon nation to establish a public program of victim compensation, preceding the British by seven months. The program in New Zealand, which began operation on January 1, 1964, is credited as having been "largely the work of Margaret Fry and the investigatory bodies in Great Britain," according to the authors of the most comprehensive work on victim-compensation legislation.[20] An alternative explanation of the implementation of the program in New Zealand was offered by Dr. J.L. Robson, Secretary of Justice. The National party had recently abolished capital punishment and was sponsoring legislation for a work-release

program for imprisoned criminals. The government offered the compensation program

as a palliative to blunt opposition to these penal reforms, as well as to respond to the public's general concern about crime. In addition, the legislation was consistent with the multitude of benefits offered citizens under the social security system.[21]

The original victim compensation program in New Zealand was similar to the program that exists in Great Britain, which will be discussed.[22] The Accident Compensation Act of 1972, which took effect April 1, 1974, eliminated the victim compensation program by absorbing it into a universal accident-compensation system. This program, which is now under consideration in Australia, "covers everyone in the country, whether resident or visitor, for any kind of accident — no matter how or when it happens or who is at fault."[23]

Coverage is so complete that about the only injury not covered by the program is one that is self-inflicted. The program pays for medical costs, incidental losses, rehabilitation and retraining, 80 percent of lost wages indefinitely, and lump sums for permanent physical disability and for pain and suffering. The family of the victim will be reimbursed for injury-related expenses and for funeral expenses, will be paid a lump sum upon the death of spouse or parent, will be paid 50 percent of wages that were earned by the deceased spouse, with extra payments for children, indefinitely or until remarriage, at which time a bonus will be given equal to two years' wage payments.[24]

No matter what the origin of the injury, with a few exceptions, the injured party files a claim with the Accident Compensation Commission. Its agents investigate claims and recommend the award to be made. Generally, moral judgments are not to be made. "The philosophy of the law isn't to look at the character of the man or the circumstances of the accident," says the commission chairman. He related one incident in which two gentlemen who injured each other in a fight were both paid for their losses.[25]

The scheme is financed by motor-vehicle registration and license fees and by a tax on employees' wages. The tax ranges from 25¢ to $5 per $100 earnings, depending upon the danger of the job. Self-employed persons are similarly assessed.[26] The first year of operation, $81 million was collected in revenues and $33 million was paid out. The commission plans to build a cash reserve to pay for claims which require payments lasting many years.[27]

Because it has so many novel aspects, and is a dramatic departure from the Anglo-Saxon tradition, the New Zealand program may provide an interesting case study in many areas in the coming years. The point of most interest to this study is whether the program will provide an added incentive to criminal activity. The following example will illustrate this issue:

Imagine for a moment you are a clumsy criminal from New York intent on

blowing open a safe here in New Zealand. You bungle the job and blow off your left thumb. . . . Two arms of the government take over. One tosses you into jail for your crime. The other pays you for your suffering. You get a check for $1,960 . . . to compensate for the lost thumb. Medical bills are paid. You probably are reimbursed for the clothes tattered by the blast. And when you get out of jail, you will be trained for work in which a missing thumb won't be missed.[28]

The Accident Compensation Act prohibits suits seeking damages for personal injuries from alleged tortfeasors. Thus, a major common-law tradition with hundreds of years of development has been felled by one act. This "mortal blow to the traditional tort system of compensating the victims of accidental injury. . ."[29] is certainly the most stunning aspect of the New Zealand plan from a legal perspective. Victim compensation, which had been introduced less than ten years before, did not single-handedly lead to this development, but was a part of it. Hence, the New Zealand experience is very important. It may provide a clue as to what may develop in other common-law countries as they also develop more public schemes for compensating various types of victims. The failures and successes of New Zealand will be providing a valuable laboratory for other common-law nations to watch in the years ahead.

As might be expected, the insurance industry was opposed to the move to public compensation in New Zealand. It is estimated that the program will eliminate 30 percent of all private insurance.[30] There is also considerable fear in the insurance industry there that the plan is the first major step in the eventual nationalization of all insurance. The government has not ruled out that possibility.[31]

Compensation in Great Britain. The most widely cited program outside of the United States has been the program in Great Britain. Following general public discussion of possible public-compensation schemes, the issue was discussed in Parliament in 1957 and 1958. In 1959 and 1960 two Labour party members introduced a "private members bill" for public compensation. In June 1961 the Home Office Working party issued a report, *Compensation for Victims of Crimes of Violence*, which examined the practical problems involved in a compensation scheme.[32]

In late 1961 the chairman of the Conservative party's Advisory Committee on Policy appointed the Committee to Consider Compensation for Injuries through Crimes of Violence. In June 1962, this committee reported favorably on compensating crime victims. The same year, the British Section of the International Commission of Jurists reported favorably on compensation, repeating the position it had taken four years previously. Favorable debate on the issue continued up to the time of adoption by the government.

In March 1964 a white paper entitled "Compensation for Victims of Crimes of Violence" was published. In May the issue was debated in the House of

Commons and the House of Lords, which produced some amendments to the proposal. In June the Home Secretary declared the program to be effective, and named the chairman of the new Criminal Injuries Compensation Board (the board). As an administrative tribunal, the executive powers of the government were sufficient to order the program into existence, and actual operations began on August 1, 1964.[33] About this time, the government issued another white paper, entitled "The War against Crime," which included numerous proposals to combat crime, including the introduction of the victim-compensation scheme. This was apparently similar to the situation in New Zealand, wherein governments perceive the need to offer compensation plans as a palliative, or as part of a larger program for the benefit of the public.[34]

The compensation program has grown rapidly since implementation, but remains relatively small by American standards. Initially the board had six members, increased to eight members by 1967, and was assisted by a staff of about forty.[35] By 1971 the board had nine members and a staff of seventy, which increased to eighty-five in 1972.[36]

Applications for compensation increased from 2,452 in the first year of full operation (1965-66), to approximately 10,000 for the fiscal year ending March 31, 1972. Compensation awards rose in that time period from £402,718 to about £3 million. Administrative costs added about 10 percent to the board's budget.[37] In fiscal 1973-74 almost £4.1 million (about $10 million) were paid to 9,024 victims of crime; £6.4 million were paid to 11,500 victims in the fiscal year ending March 31, 1976. Hence, the average compensation payment has been about $1,000, in a country which has socialized medicine and a lower standard of living than the United States. During fiscal 1975-76, 17 percent of the awards were to policemen. Most payments are made on a rule-of-thumb basis. A broken nose is worth £200-300; a broken jaw worth £450; a stab in the chest which requires surgery will net £650; a rape victim who has no lasting physical or psychological reactions will receive £1,000; and the loss of one eye will result in a £5,000 compensation award.[38]

One author estimated that the ten thousand applications the Board received in the early 1970s represented about one-third of the total number of victims available. Board researchers concluded in the late 1960s that "the maximum number of applications we could ever expect to receive (subject, of course, to any startling increase in crime) is between 16,000 and 18,500."[39] These expectations were surpassed in fiscal 1976-77, when an estimated 20,000 applications were filed. The number will be held down by a board decision in 1977 to increase the minimum award from £50 to £150.[40]

The compensation procedure is less legalistic than it is in some jurisdictions. Applications may be submitted by the applicant in person. More commonly, however, they are submitted on a form supplied by the board. Although application forms are available only from the Board, police stations and other agencies have copies of the program and procedural guides.[41] A little more than half

of the applicants are represented by a lawyer or by trade-union officials. Those represented by a lawyer must pay for his assistance; however, their success rate for receiving compensation is much higher than that of the nonrepresented individuals.[42]

New applications are received by staff members, who act as caseworkers on each application they process. The caseworker makes sure the application is complete and gathers whatever information he believes is needed to prepare the case for consideration. Since there are no formal rules of evidence, work is done on a basis of voluntary cooperation with public officials, medical authorities, and witnesses. "In general, it is the caseworking officer's duty to see that all relevant matters are brought to the attention of the board member whether they are in the applicant's favor or to his detriment."[43]

When all inquiries have been completed the staff member prepares a summary that, with the application and all other relevant materials, is sent to a single member of the board. Members receive, in rotation, batches of ten cases. The member makes his own assessment of the application, and can accept or reject the application, or make a smaller award. The decision is then returned to the caseworker, who notifies the applicant of the decision, which can be accepted or rejected. About 90 percent of the single-member decisions are accepted, each having an administrative cost of about £25 on the average, compared to the £120 average cost incurred in each appeal (in 1972).[44]

When an appeal is made it will be heard by three other members of the board. Their decision will rest solely on the evidence given at the hearing, which is open for review by the applicant. The report used in the single member's decision is not used as evidence. A new investigation of the case provides evidence for presentation in a closed hearing, one not bound by normal court procedures. The applicant is represented by a lawyer about half the time. If there is no lawyer for the applicant, then the board's lawyer acts as *amicus curiae*, presenting all relevant facts and arguments, whether favorable or unfavorable to the applicant's case.[45] The three-man board makes an assessment completely independent of the initial, single member's decision, so that a claimant may have his award reduced. However, in 80 percent of the appeals the award is increased in value.[46]

In a case brought against the board after a three-man ruling, the court ruled that the board is not exempt "from the supervisory control by the High Court over that part of their functions which is judicial in character." Therefore, to this extent the board is subject to an "appeal" to the courts; in other respects the decision of the board consequent upon a hearing is, of course, "final."[47]

The board has changed little in Great Britain since its inception. There has been some criticism of the awards assessments, which are low by American standards, and of the fact that the state does not provide applicants with free legal assistance.[48] However, the program is broader in scope than most, and provides compensation for some damages that many programs do not. Except

for a £150 deductible, "compensation in injury cases is paid both for pain and suffering, disfigurement and the impairment of the enjoyment or activities of life, and for loss of earnings past and prospective and the out-of-pocket expenses incurred as the result of the injury."[49]

Due to a development unrelated to the compensation program, it has become easier for victims of crime to receive some restitution from their assailants. The Theft Act of 1968 conferred wide powers of restitution on the court, and gave limited powers to award restitution directly from the criminal to cover the property damages suffered by their victims. A criminal-court judge can order a criminal to return stolen goods or, if it is not possible to return them, to collect funds from the criminal equal to the value of the goods or the property damage.[50]

Similarly, the Civil Evidence Act of 1968, which provides that the conviction of an offender is admissible evidence in civil proceedings, has made it easier for a victim of property loss to receive restitution for the loss. "In practical terms, therefore, once the offender is convicted, that conviction will in the majority of cases be ample corroboration to obtain a civil judgment, and indeed in the majority of cases it would seem unlikely that civil proceedings would be defended."[51] This contrasts with American courts, where the existence of a criminal conviction is legally unrelated to any civil proceedings taken by the victim to recover property losses.

The Criminal Damage Act of 1971, the Criminal Justice Act of 1972, and the Powers of Criminal Courts Act of 1973 have provided English courts with increased powers to require criminals to pay restitution to their victims.[52] The payment is not to exceed £400 if the conviction is in a magistrate's court.[53] The restitution order is "in respect of any personal injury, loss or damage from an offence for which the defendant is convicted...."[54] Such orders are not strictly parts of sentences given; they are ancillary to the sentences.

As in most jurisdictions which have provided the courts the power to make such orders, the usage has been limited in practice by the judges. According to one observer, the courts provide for limited payments based upon ability of the criminal to pay and do not require payments when the criminal has been sentenced to prison.[55] Another observer noted that few cases have emerged under these laws, and awards have been limited to small weekly payments which usually are for less than the damage done. The judges are supposedly concerned that the defendant will turn to crime in order to fulfill a restitution order.[56] "One general rule emerges very clearly indeed: the scheme was devised to meet simple cases where no great sums of money are at stake."[57] If such is to be the case, then it appears that the judges will not go far to make restitution by the criminal replace compensation provided by the state.

Compensation in Northern Ireland. Victim compensation in Northern Ireland is interesting, not because the program is significantly different from that in

Great Britain, but because it may provide a subsidy for the violent internal strife that has plagued Northern Ireland in the 1970s.

First it is worth considering the compensation scheme that existed in what is now the nation of Ireland at the time of the Irish revolution. The Easter Rising of 1916 marked the beginnings of the revolution which continued for about the next six years. Ireland gained independence in December of 1921 and was allowed to withdraw from dominion status in December of 1922. Property damage that was suffered during the revolution could be compensated under traditional Irish law. One could receive compensation from county governments for property damages due to riots and other acts that were noninsurable by private means.

Due to the extensive damages inflicted during the revolution, county governments soon became unwilling and unable to pay court-ordered compensation awards. This led to the Criminal Injuries (Ireland) Act of 1920

by which it was enacted that a decree against a county council under any enactment relating to compensation for criminal injuries was to be a debt due, and that it was to be the duty of the County Treasurer to pay the amount on demand, or out of the first monies coming into his hands, whether raised as compensation or not.[58]

This led to a great burden on county governments to meet the compensation due, so that following the revolution the Irish central government and the British government agreed to pay the compensation claims.[59]

The county-compensation scheme came under similar pressure in Northern Ireland due to cross-border raids in the late 1950s. The Criminal Injuries Act (Northern Ireland) of 1956 stipulated that the Ministry of Home Affairs would reimburse local governments for 50 percent of the compensation payments awarded. The burden continued to be so great, however, that the Criminal Injuries Act (Northern Ireland) of 1957 allowed for the Ministry of Home Affairs to reimburse county councils for compensation payments made for property damage "caused by a malicious person acting on behalf of an unlawful association."[60] This act, which was extended on an annual basis until it was made permanent in 1970, imposes "collective responsibility for civil disorder resulting in damage to property."[61]

The Criminal Injuries to Property (Compensation) Act (Northern Ireland) of 1971 provides for all claims to be made directly to the Ministry for Home Affairs. In the four-year period encompassing 1969 through 1972 there were almost 50,000 claims for malicious damage compensation, totaling £50 million. During that time "15,648 claims had been disposed of and £25,185,269 paid in compensation.[62] Hence, the government paid out approximately $60 million directly to victims of property damage due to the conflict in Northern Ireland.

The Criminal Injuries to Persons (Compensation) Act (Northern Ireland)

of 1968 inaugurated compensation for criminal injuries. This program is comprehensive, providing awards through the county courts for personal injuries attributable to criminal behavior. Coverage is so complete that if a cyclist is injured by a dog on the road, the cyclist will receive compensation because the loose dog violated the leash law, so that injury was caused by a criminal offense. [63]

Compensation is for all injuries, including bodily harm, pregnancy, and mental or nervous shock, due to direct assault or incurred in attempting to prevent a crime or assist an officer in an arrest. All expenses incurred by the victim and/or his dependents, including pain and suffering and loss of amenities, will be awarded by the court. In case of death or disability, besides the expenses incurred, total annual income for up to two years will be awarded. [64]

This coverage, as broad as any offered anywhere, was a great expansion of the limited compensation that had been available in Northern Ireland since 1775. It provided that one would be compensated if a person had been killed or injured "as the result of the activity of an illegal association or unlawful assembly."[65]

The Northern Ireland Criminal Injuries Act provides that any person convicted of a criminal offense may be required, upon application by the Ministry of Home Affairs, to reimburse the ministry in part or in whole for the compensation awarded by the county court. This procedure leads to a court review of the case and assessment against the offender based on his ability to pay, his financial position, the possibility of future employment, and the liabilities to his family.[66] How much this feature is in fact used in practice is unknown. If it is used as little as it is in other jurisdictions that have this procedure, then it is likely to be insignificant in impact.

In contrast to most jurisdictions, in which compensation payments are akin to a welfare payment, "it is now well settled that the local authority is to be considered to be in the position of a tortfeasor."[67] The state has replaced the criminal as the party responsible for damage inflicted in civil strife. As a result of this legislation, one expert hypothesizes that civil strife in Northern Ireland may be correlated with victim compensation.[68] He notes that political disturbances worsened following the introduction of that program in 1969. "Such legislation in Ireland can patently be shown to be indissolubly connected with its recent political history."[69]

Australian Compensation Schemes. Advocates of governmental compensation are often unhappy with the compensation plans that have emerged in some Australian states. Beginning with the Criminal Injuries Compensation Act in 1967 in New South Wales, three other states, Queensland, South Australia, and Western Australia, followed in the next three years with compensation plans. In Victoria a victim can apply for compensation from a special Crimes Compensation Tribunal. As of 1974 Tasmania was considering adoption of the New South Wales scheme.[70]

The statutory basis for the New South Wales plan is in the Crimes Act of 1900 and the Criminal Injuries Compensation Act of 1967. The 1900 act gave courts the power to pay a sum, not exceeding $2,000, out of the property of a convicted offender to his victim for the loss or injury sustained by the commission of the felony or misdemeanor.[71] In cases of courts of summary jurisdiction, the award was not to exceed $300. The 1967 act extended the 1900 act so that, if the funds could not be extracted from the offender, the court could award compensation via the state treasury, subject to approval by the treasurer.[72]

Since the 1900 act was almost never used, the 1967 act is novel in effect. Although the courts may extract payments from the offender, subject to his ability to pay, as of 1971 less than one percent of the total payments to victims had been paid by the offender.[73] Initially, eligibility for compensation was to be coincident with the conviction of the criminal, but the Attorney-General of New South Wales subsequently ruled that *ex gratia* payments could be made to all crime victims.[74]

Somewhat similar to the New South Wales case, the Queensland Criminal Code provides that a first-offender may, upon suspension of the execution of his sentence, be ordered to make restitution to his victim to pay for the damages inflicted, in lump sum or installments. Queensland judges have "quite frequently included an order for payment of compensation as one of the requirements of a probation order."[75] Most Australian states allow for compensation of individuals who are injured in attempts to assist the police in preventing a crime or apprehending a criminal.[76]

The Australian compensation schemes were passed into law primarily for two reasons. First, it was assumed that violent crime had increased rapidly in the 1960s, and that there were numerous compensable injuries. Second, existing laws were considered defunct in almost never providing victim compensation through restitution by the criminal or by tort action.[77]

In the Australian scheme the method of administering compensation may create a conflict of interest within the prosecutor's office. The prosecutor not only is charged with presenting the state's case against the offender, but also is charged with rebutting the victim's claim for damages. The prosecution is supposed to expose the true extent of injuries, which could give the impression that the victim is unreliable or not as grievously injured as claimed, so that the case against the criminal could be biased.[78] Of course it would be desirable for the prosecutor to expose unreliable victims. It is not clear whether or not this has been a problem in practice.

Compensation in Canada. Victim-compensation programs exist in at least eight of the ten Canadian provinces.[79] A 1967 report issued by the Legislative Committee of the Canadian Corrections Association urged national adoption of victim compensation, including compensation for property losses. "Offenses committed by a member of the victim's family upon him and losses from motor

vehicle injuries were both included within the proposed compensation approach."[80] This contrasts with the almost uniform exclusion of these two classes of offenses in existing compensation programs, as well as the usual exclusion of property losses. The committee also urged that grants be given to individuals who were erroneously prosecuted or convicted of any offense. Although compensation was adopted in numerous provinces, none of the unusual features advocated by the Canadian Corrections Association was adopted.

Saskatchewan initiated compensation in Canada, proclaiming the Criminal Injuries Compensation Act on September 1, 1967, but retroactive in effect to one year before that date. The program was generally modeled after the initial New Zealand approach, creating a three-man board to have absolute discretion over all cases, with no appeal to courts possible. Few bounds are placed on the awards that may be made to victims who have suffered injuries in a crime, in attempting to prevent a crime, or in attempting to assist a policeman in preventing a crime or making an arrest. There is a $50 minimum on awards and a stipulation that any awards over $5,000 must be approved by the lieutenant governor. There are the usual rules about contributory negligence reducing the amount of the award, a statute of limitations on making claims, and the like, but lump-sum or periodic payments can be awarded for all nonproperty expenses incurred, for pain and suffering, and for losses due to disability or death.[81]

As in some of the Australian states, the Saskatchewan attorney general may sue a criminal for the amount of compensation awarded by the board to his victim, if the victim did not sue the criminal for civil damages. This power is at the discretion of the attorney general, who must take into account the financial status of the criminal and any family responsibilities he may have.[82] If the experience is like that of other jurisdictions with this rule, it will be used rarely.

The compensation schemes in the other provinces do not differ greatly from the Saskatchewan plan, except in some details which are noted here. Ontario is the only province that does not provide an explicit list of offenses for which compensation can be granted. So long as an individual is the victim of a criminal offense, he may receive an award. Ontario is also the only province which places no minimum on the compensation that may be requested.[83] Ontario and New Brunswick are the only provinces allowing compensation for property loss, but only when the loss is the consequence of attempting to perform a lawful arrest, preventing a crime, or assisting a police officer. Only Ontario permits all questions of law to be appealed to the high court, and allows review by use of the prerogative writs.[84]

The only province which administers claims through hearings by a judge of the county court is New Brunswick.[85] It also has an unusual provision that allows the recovery of about 10 percent of the benefits received from insurance sources, on the ground that this amount represents the cost of the victim's insurance premiums.[86]

Compensation for pain and suffering is not allowed in Manitoba and Quebec because the schemes are tied to the provinces' Workmen's Compensation Act. Benefits under these acts do not allow recovery for pain and suffering.[87] This means that in Manitoba a victim can receive up to three-quarters of the minimum wage in effect in that province (about $8,000 in 1972) plus their medical expenses. If victims remain permanently disabled, they may receive a pension for the remainder of their lives.[88] Manitoba, Alberta, and British Columbia provide expenses for rehabilitating the applicant for employment purposes.

Alberta and Manitoba allow appeals to the Queen's Bench on jurisdictional questions and matters of law. Like Saskatchewan, these provinces have no statutory limit on the size of awards. Like Newfoundland and Saskatchewan, Alberta grants the right to legal counsel to anyone appearing before the board.[89] The executive secretary of the Crime Victim Compensation Board in Alberta told delegates to the Third International Conference on the Compensation of Victims of Crime (1972) that ". . .unfortunately, 80 percent of our applicants in Alberta tell lies," presumably in an attempt to increase the size of their compensation awards.[90] (The 80 percent figure appears to be a pure guess and is not substantiated.) Other delegates noted similar problems.

The programs in British Columbia and Quebec are similar. Both are based on their Workmen's Compensation Act and are administered by the Workmen's Compensation Board or Commission. These provinces require that the applicant elect either to pursue any possible civil remedy or apply for compensation.[91] An unusual feature of the Quebec plan is "that the commission may grant an annuity to the mother of a child born as a result of rape if she provides for the maintenance of the child."[92]

Newfoundland's program, which went into effect in April 1972, is modeled on the compensation system in Saskatchewan. Its only unusual aspect is the small size of the maximum award that may be granted, either $1,000 in a lump sum or $30 a month in periodic payments.[93]

In 1973 federal subsidization of the provinces' programs was implemented. The central government will pay the lesser of the following amounts: (1) five cents per annum per person living in the province, or (2) not more than 90 percent of the total compensation granted, excluding awards for pain and suffering and administrative expenses. It has been estimated that this plan will cover half of the costs of the program in Ontario.[94]

A judicial development of interest, common to Canada and England, is that the courts have agreed that a person may recover compensation for nervous shock sustained as the result of witnessing a criminal attack upon a relative, or "as a result of witnessing the aftermath of the crime," such as from receiving the news of one's son's murder.[95]

Compensation in Non-English Nations. Few non-English-speaking countries have victim-compensation programs, probably because many have such extensive social-welfare programs that compensation would be mostly repetitive, and

because they do not have common-law tort and criminal-law procedures, which has made restitution difficult. A survey of twenty-nine countries in the late 1950s revealed that only Pakistan and India (former British colonies) and the common-law nations completely separate civil from criminal proceedings, so that victims were required to bear the burden of seeking payment from the criminal without state assistance.[96] In most other countries the victims could ask for restitution from the criminal as a part of the criminal proceedings.

In pre-Castro Cuba, the state would award compensation to victims, then seek indemnification from criminals. The courts appeared to have been quite strict in recovering from criminals, so that the indemnity fund was substantial but never sufficient to cover all claims.[97] This idea has been considered in the United States, as will be seen. In Switzerland, victims could appeal for restitution from criminals. Failing that, they could seek compensation from the state, but this was little used in practice.[98]

The survey found that many nations effectively bar victims from enforcing claims against criminals imprisoned, despite the fact that the criminals may be earning wages in prison (Holland, Finland, New Zealand, Norway, India, Pakistan, Germany, and Austria). Most nations do allow victims to enforce claims against criminals now imprisoned (Canada, Denmark, Israel, Italy, Sweden, Turkey, and the United States). France and the Dominican Republic take positive steps to force prisoners to pay their victims.[99]

Among the recent developments is included the institution of a small compensation program in Sweden in 1971, which was supposedly due to increases in crime. Due to comprehensive insurance schemes in that country, in practice the compensation applies only to a small percent of the population and to visitors to the country. There was some discussion of implementing similar programs in Norway and Finland.[100]

On January 30, 1976, the West German parliament passed a law which will allow victims to collect up to about $19,000 for personal injury or property damage, whenever the costs are not covered by insurance, the attacker is unknown, or the attacker is unable to pay restitution. Compensation will also be paid to individuals who suffer losses assisting victims of crime or victims of automobile accidents.[101]

Support for victim compensation around the world was evidenced by the conclusions and recommendations adopted by the First International Symposium on Victimology, which included the resolution that "All nations should, as a matter or urgency, give consideration to the establishment of state systems of compensation for victims of crime. . . ."[102]

Notes

1. Chilperic Edwards, *The Hammurabi Code* (Port Washington, New York: Kennikat Press, 1971), p. 31.

2. Arthur J. Goldberg, "Preface" (Symposium on Victim Compensation), *Southern California Law Review* 43 (1970), p.1.

3. Henry S. Maine, *Ancient Law* (London: John Murray, 11th ed., 1887), p. 370.

4. Ibid.

5. Ibid.

6. Ibid., p. 374.

7. Ibid.

8. Ibid., p. 378.

9. Christopher Hibbert, *The Roots of Evil* (New York: Funk & Wagnalls, 1968), p.3.

10. Maine, *Ancient Law*, p. 381.

11. Ibid., p. 397.

12. Ibid., p. 399.

13. Richard Laster, "Criminal Restitution," *University of Richmond Law Review* 5 (Fall 1970), pp. 75-79.

14. Edwin Powers, *Crime and Punishment in Early Massachusetts, 1620-1692* (Boston: Beacon Press, 1966), pp. 404-408.

15. Ibid., p. 410.

16. Richard Worsnop, "Compensation for Victims of Crime," *Editorial Research Reports,* 22 (September 1965), p. 696.

17. Raffaele Garofalo, *Criminology* (1905; Montclair, N.J.: Patterson Smith, reprinted ed., 1958), p. 434.

18. Margaret Fry, *The Arms of the Law* (1951), cited in Bruce Jacob, "Reparation or Restitution by the Criminal Offender to His Victim," *Journal of Criminal Law, Criminology and Police Science* 61 (1970), p. 152.

19. Margaret Fry, "Justice for Victims," *The Observer* (London), July 7, 1957, cited in Jacob, "Reparation or Restitution," p. 152.

20. Herbert Edelhertz and Gilbert Geis, *Public Compensation to Victims of Crime* (New York· Praeger Publishers, Inc. 1974), p. 238.

21. Kent M. Weeks, "The New Zealand Criminal Injuries Compensation Board," *Southern California Law Review* 43 (1970), p. 108.

22. Peter Brett, "Compensation for the Victims of Crime: New Zealand's Pioneer Statute," *Australian Lawyer* 5 (March 1964), pp. 21-27.

23. "To Accident Victims, New Zealand Offers the Balm of Money," *Wall Street Journal,* September 16, 1975, p. 1.

24. J.L. Fahy, "The Administration of the Accident Compensation Act 1972," *Economic Bulletin,* Canterbury Chamber of Commerce, no. 592 (Christchurch, N.Z., 1975), sec. 5.

25. "New Zealand Offers the Balm of Money," *Wall Street Journal,* p.1.

26. Fahy, "The Accident Compensation Act 1972," sec. 4.

27. Dollar amounts are New Zealand dollars, which are worth a little more than U.S. dollars. It is interesting to note that New Zealand, long recognized as a welfare state, only recently adopted old-age social security. The program is

more flexible than the American program. An employee can opt to be covered by a company plan and can also vary the contribution from his wages if he uses the government plan. "New Zealand Offers the Balm of Money," *Wall Street Journal*, p. 1.

28. Ibid.

29. Geoffrey Palmer, "Compensation for Personal Injury: A Requiem for the Common Law in New Zealand," *American Journal of Comparative Law*, 21 (1973), p. 1.

30. Ibid., p. 42.

31. Ibid., pp. 42-43.

32. Edelhertz and Geis, *Public Compensation*, p. 214.

33. Ibid., pp. 214-15.

34. Duncan Chappell, "The Emergence of Australian Schemes to Compensate Victims of Crime," *Southern California Law Review* 43 (1970), p. 70.

35. "Recent Legislative Action," *Harvard Law Review* 78 (June 1965), p. 1684; J.F. Garner, "The Criminal Injuries Compensation Board," *Public Law* (1967), p. 323.

36. David H. Harrison, "Criminal Injuries Compensation in Britain," *American Bar Association Journal* 57 (May 1971), p. 476. Edelhertz and Geis, *Public Compensation*, p. 216.

37. Edelhertz and Geis, *Public Compensation*, p. 232, citing Criminal Compensation Board, *Annual Reports*, 1965-1971; *The Times* (London), November 12, 1971, p. 3; and *New York Times*, November 29, 1972, p. 2.

38. *The Times* (London), February 3, 1976, p. 5; February 16, 1977, p. 4; D. Miers and E. Veitch, "Assault on the Law of Tort," *Modern Law Review* 38 (March 1975), p. 148.

39. Alec Samuels, "Criminal Injuries Compensation Board," *Criminal Law Review* (July 1973), p. 418; Criminal Injuries Compensation Board, *Fourth Report*, cmnd. 3814, 1968, cited in Edelhertz and Geis, *Public Compensation*, p. 225.

40. *The Times* (London), February 16, 1977, p. 4.

41. Garner, "Compensation Board," p. 324.

42. Samuels, "Criminal Injuries Compensation Board," p. 419.

43. Harrison, "Compensation in Britain," p. 478.

44. Samuels, "Criminal Injuries Compensation Board," p. 429.

45. Harrison, "Compensation in Britain," p. 479.

46. Samuels, "Criminal Injuries Compensation Board," p. 429.

47. Garner, "Compensation Board," p. 329, citing R. *Criminal Injuries Compensation Board, ex p. Lain* (1967), 2 All E.R. 770, at p. 781.

48. J.C. Walker, "Valuations of the Criminal Injuries Compensation Board," *The Solicitors' Journal* 110 (December 30, 1966), pp. 970-71.

49. Harrison, "Compensation in Britain," p. 477.

50. Terence Prime, "Reparation from the Offender - I," *The Solicitors' Journal* 115 (November 19, 1971), pp. 859-61.

51. Terence Prime, "Reparation from the Offender - II," *The Solicitors' Journal* 115 (November 26, 1971), pp. 880-82.

52. Michael Robinson and Gianluca la Villa, "English Criminal Courts and Compensation Orders," *Anglo-American Law Review* 4 (November 3, 1975), pp. 345-48; J.L. Lambert, "Compensation Orders—A Review of Appellate Cases—I—II," *New Law Journal* 126 (January 8, 15, 1976), pp. 47-48, 69-70.

53. Lambert, "Compensation Orders," p. 47.

54. Robinson, "English Criminal Courts," p. 346.

55. Lambert, "Compensation Orders," p. 48.

56. Robinson, "English Criminal Courts," p. 347.

57. Lambert, "Compensation Orders," p. 70.

58. D.R. Miers, "Paying for Malicious Injuries Claims," *Irish Jurist* 5 (Summer 1970), p. 56.

59. Ibid., pp. 58-59.

60. Ibid, p. 63.

61. W.C.H. Ervine, "Compensation for Malicious Damage to Property," *New Law Journal* 123 (May 24, 1973), p. 497.

62. Ibid.

63. D.R. Miers, "Compensation for Victims of Crime of Violence: The Northern Ireland Model," *Criminal Law Review* (November 1969), pp. 577-78.

64. Subject to an original limitation of £44 10s. per week, an amount double the average weekly earnings for men over age twenty-one.

65. Miers, "Compensation for Victims," pp. 578-79.

66. Ibid., p. 585.

67. Ervine, "Compensation for Malicious Damage," p. 497.

68. Miers, "Compensation for Victims," p. 583.

69. Ibid.

70. W.T. Westling, "Some Aspects of the Judicial Determination of Compensation Payable to Victims of Crime," *Australian Law Journal* 48 (September 1974), p. 428.

71. Maximum award was increased to $4,000 in 1972. All dollar sums are Australian dollars, A.$1 equals U.S. $1.12, approximately.

72. Duncan Chappell, "Compensating Australian Victims of Violent Crime," *Australian Law Journal* 41 (May 31, 1967), p. 9.

73. K.M. McCaw, "Report on the New South Wales Criminal Injuries Compensation Act," in *The Australian Criminal Justice System*, Duncan Chappell and Paul Wilson, eds. (Australia: Butterworth, 1972), p. 785.

74. Chappell, "Emergence of Australian Schemes," p. 73.

75. P.R. Delemothe, "Victim Compensation: The Queensland Scheme," in *The Australian Criminal Justice System*, p. 792.

76. For example, see "Police Assistance Compensation Act 1968 (Victoria)," in *The Australian Criminal Justice System*, pp. 795-97.

77. Chappell, "Emergence of Australian Schemes," pp. 76-77.

78. Chappell, "Compensating Australian Victims," pp. 9-10.

79. In order of implementation: Saskatchewan, Ontario, New Brunswick, Manitoba, Alberta, British Columbia, Quebec, and Newfoundland.

80. Edelhertz and Geis, *Public Compensation*, p. 242.

81. James Eremko, "Compensation of Criminal Injuries in Saskatchewan," *University of Toronto Law Journal* 19 (1969), pp. 263-76.

82. Ibid., pp. 269-70.

83. Edelhertz and Geis, *Public Compensation*, pp. 244-45.

84. Peter Burns and Alan M. Ross, "A Comparative Study of Victims of Crime Indemnification in Canada," *University of British Columbia Law Review* 8 (November 1, 1973), pp. 124-25, 127-28.

85. Ibid., p. 127.

86. Edelhertz and Geis, *Public Compensation*, p. 246.

87. Burns and Ross, "A Comparative Study," pp. 124, 126.

88. Edelhertz and Geis, *Public Compensation*, p. 246.

89. Burns and Ross, "A Comparative Study," pp. 126-28.

90. Edelhertz and Geis, *Public Compensation*, pp. 246-47.

91. Burns and Ross, "A Comparative Study," pp. 126-28.

92. Edelhertz and Geis, *Public Compensation*, p. 247.

93. Burns and Ross, "A Comparative Study," p. 126.

94. Edelhertz and Geis, *Public Compensation*, p. 247.

95. D.R. Miers, "The Ontario Criminal Injuries Compensation Scheme," *University of Toronto Law Journal* 24 (Autumn 1974), p. 357.

96. Stephen Schafer, *Restitution to Victims of Crime* (Chicago: Quadrangle Books Inc., 1960), p. 103.

97. Ibid., pp. 66-72.

98. Ibid., p. 106.

99. Ibid., p. 107.

100. Edelhertz and Geis, *Public Compensation*, pp. 250-51.

101. *Miami Herald*, January 31, 1975, p. 11.

102. Israel Drapkin and Emilio Viano, eds., *Victimology: A New Focus* (Lexington, Mass.: Lexington Books, 1974), p. 210. The reader should remember that those voting for this resolution would generally stand to gain in a personal sense by its adoption.

3 American Compensation Plans

State Compensation Programs

California. California was the first American state, and the third Anglo-Saxon jurisdiction, to implement a plan for compensating victims of crime. Perhaps because the program was passed into law before the first federal legislation was proposed, the California scheme was unusual compared to the programs adopted by all other states, which benefited from the existence of the victim-compensation bill before Congress.

Enacted during the 1965 legislative session, the compensation program began operation the first of 1966. Part of the legislation was a "Good Samaritan" provision that allowed citizens injured in aiding in the apprehension of a criminal or in the prevention of a crime to appeal to the state board of control for compensation for all costs incurred.[1] This provision was essentially unrelated to the victim-compensation scheme and has not become significant. In the seven fiscal years from 1967 through 1974 only 101 grants, totaling $272,947, were awarded.[2]

The compensation portion of the legislation was placed within the jurisdiction of the state department of social welfare. It was instructed to

establish criteria for the payment of aid substantially the same as those used in the program for aid to families with dependent children (AFDC). Crime victims, however, need not meet the property qualifications of AFDC.[3]

To qualify, a victim had to show that he was incapacitated and that his family income fell below a certain level. The program, therefore, provided monthly assistance to individuals meeting the proper qualifications, but did not provide medical or hospital care, or any other expenses directly associated with the crime suffered.

To help finance the program the bill established an indemnity fund, which required that:

Upon conviction of a person of a crime of violence resulting in the injury or death of another person, the court shall take into consideration the defendant's economic condition, and. . .shall, in addition to any other penalty, order the defendant to pay a fine commensurate with the offense committed. The fine shall be deposited in the Indemnity Fund, in the State Treasury, and the proceeds in such fund shall be used for payment of aid under this section.[4]

In the first year of operation of the indemnity fund (1966) a total of $5,200 was received from six offenders.[5] The initial enthusiasm of California judges in applying this provision apparently waned. In fiscal 1971-72, $50 was collected. Nothing was collected in fiscal 1972-73.[6]

Upon enactment, the director of the department of social welfare announced that the duty of administering the program was "improperly placed," and claimed that his department would only provide assistance to those in "need" (those who fully qualified for AFDC).[7] The director's indignation was further aroused by the first year's appropriation of $100,000, which he stated was "like telling us to go out and buy a steak and giving us 35 cents to do it with."[8] However, the director managed not to overspend his budget. In November 1967 the entire program was turned over to the state board of control.

The board of control acts as an administrative tribunal. A staff prepares the cases for review and decision by the board, which decrees the awards. Hearings, not bound by the rules and procedures of a court, are held by the board or by appointed hearing officers, who recommend action to the board. While all decisions rendered by the board are subject to legislative approval, in practice this is generally a rubber-stamp approval.[9]

Amending legislation in October 1973 (effective July 1, 1974) increased the maximum award to $10,000 for medical expenses, $10,000 for lost income, and $3,000 for employment rehabilitation expenses. The board is also authorized to pay attorneys' fees, not exceeding 10 percent of the award, or $500, whichever is less.[10] Some observers consider the attorney fees to be quite generous considering the small amount of work required in filing claims.[11]

Despite California's size, its compensation program remains relatively small. This may be attributed to "the absence of a separate administrative board and the inclusion of the hardship requirement,. . ." an arrangement peculiar to California.[12] Through the first eleven months of the 1976-1977 fiscal year the state board of control had allowed 2,284 claims for almost $4.4 million. Payments to victims, including attorneys' fees, have averaged slightly under $2,000 for the past several years.[13]

In 1974 the attorney general of California sent a letter to all local law-enforcement agencies in the state. He notified them that, since less than one percent of all victims of a violent crime were applying for benefits, by the terms of the new amendments to the victim-compensation program, they were to begin informing all victims of the existence of the program.[14] From July 1974 to July 1977 the program approximately tripled in size, so that only a very small percent of victims are still helped by the program.

New York. On October 9, 1965, Arthur F. Collins attempted to prevent a drunk from bothering several elderly women on a New York City subway car, and was stabbed to death while his wife looked on. This case received considerable

attention in the press, and helped to stimulate the adoption of victim compensation in New York. The New York program is similar to the program adopted in most states implementing compensation for victims. As such, it can stand as a model for the typical state compensation program.

Five weeks after Collins's murder, the New York City Council passed a "Good Samaritan" statute, which "authorized awards for the death or injury of any person other than a peace officer caused during an attempt on a public street or in a city-owned transit facility to prevent a crime or to preserve the peace."[15] Loss of earnings, medical expenses, and, in case of death, an award to surviving dependents would be provided.

Two weeks after Collins's death, Governor Rockefeller endorsed the victim-compensation concept and established a committee to study its feasibility for adoption by the 1966 legislative session. The first bills introduced in both houses of the legislature in 1966 were compensation measures. The proposal recommended by Rockefeller's committee was presented in April 1966; the measure easily passed the legislature in July of that year, and went into effect in March 1967.[16]

The Crime Victims Compensation Board was established to operate the New York program. The original three-man board was increased to five members in 1973, to help with the increasing claims load.[17] By 1973 the board had established three offices, in Albany, New York City, and Buffalo, to facilitate the handling of claims. Staff invesitgators process claims, preparing the cases for consideration by the board.[18] Decisions are rendered by individual board members but are subject to appeal to the full board, as happens in about 10 percent of all cases. Appeal by the attorney general or the controller is possible, but has never occurred.[19]

Compensation for pain and suffering is not allowed, as the law limits awards to out-of-pocket expenses plus loss of earnings or support resulting from the injury sustained. However, compensation is not allowed unless the board is "convinced that the claimant will incur 'serious financial hardship' in the event that compensation is withheld."[20] The interpretation of the hardship test is left to the discretion of the board members. Like California, New York joins about half of the states which have victim compensation in the hardship test. This undoubtedly has contributed to the relatively small size of the New York program.

Like most states, New York has a $100 deductible from awards, intended to reduce the volume of small claims. The maximum award, in case of loss of earnings, is up to $135 a week until a maximum of $15,000 is reached. There is no maximum for medical expenses. Although these provisions are more generous than provided by most states, the board would like to increase the maximum payments for loss of earnings.[21]

Attorneys' fees are set by the board and are paid out of the award. Less than one in five claimants is represented by a lawyer. This may be due to the

size of the awards, which are generally small and are based on the "amount of work actually done for the claimant," not upon the size of award obtained for the claimant.[22] It is likely that, just as some attorneys have come to specialize in workmen's-compensation cases, some will specialize in victim compensation, which will lead to more representation of claimants.

The program has changed little since its inception, despite attempts to alter its scope. Various bills before the legislature have proposed compensation for pain and suffering, compensation for property damages resulting from crime, and compensation to churches for damages suffered by vandalism, bombing, or arson.[23]

In January 1976, Governor Carey appointed a new chairman of the Crime Victims Compensation Board with instructions to reform the program. The new chairman reported to the governor that he has acted "with alacrity," primarily through changes in "bureaucratic procedures."[24] The claim form has been simplified; it is distributed by police departments and other interested agencies; it is to be acted upon by an investigator with fifteen days (who is to help document the claim); and it is to be processed more quickly than had been the usual practice. Several investigators have been reassigned from fraud investigation to claim servicing.[25]

In the fiscal year ending March 31, 1976, $3 million was paid to crime victims.[26] Since administrative expenses were about 20 percent of the New York budget in 1975, total expenditures in 1976 were about $3.75 million. The average award in 1975 was slightly over $2,000.[27]

Even within the confines of the financial-requirements test (serious financial hardship), there is a good potential for growth of the New York program. It was estimated that in 1973 3 percent of the victims of violent crime in New York City were eligible for compensation, but only 20 percent of those eligible filed for an award.[28] To help expand the program, besides the procedural changes undertaken, the board has suggested amendments to the legislature for the program which would: (1) have the board pay attorneys in addition to awards; (2) repeal the financial-hardship test; (3) extend coverage to minors injured or killed by family members; (4) allow the board and attorney general to compromise subrogation claims; (5) require defendants convicted of certain crimes to pay minimal monetary penalties, which would help finance the compensation program; and (6) require the police to notify all victims of crime of the Crime Victims Compensation Law.[29]

It is possible that the New York program is basically in a holding operation, like other states' programs, awaiting passage of the federal legislation which would subsidize operations. This was noted a few years ago by the chairman, who looked "with an eye to the impending enactment of the Federal Crime Victims Compensation legislation. . ." because "the board will then be able to enlarge the number of claims eligible to receive awards."[30]

Maryland. Inaugurating its program on July 1, 1968, following its passage into law in May 1968 by Governor Spiro Agnew, Maryland has had one of the largest and most active victim-compensation programs among the states. Despite a financial-hardship requirement, the Criminal Injuries Compensation Board has gradually expanded its program over the years. In fiscal 1975-76 the board awarded $1.7 million (projected to rise to $1.9 million the next year). There were 413 awards, so the average value of an award was over $4,000.[31]

Except for 1974 and half of 1975, when there was no upper limit on awards, the largest award possible has remained at $45,000.[32] Attorneys, representing 90 percent of all claimants, usually collect between 10 and 20 percent of the award, out of the award granted, as determined by the board. The largest attorney fee was $3,000, while between $225 and $275 is paid for a $1,500 award.[33]

There are three basic categories of awards: (1) lump-sum payments, where the claimant can return to work; (2) protracted payments, where monthly support is provided during disability; and (3) death payments, where monthly support is made to the dependents of the victim. The awards are generally based upon the workmen's-compensation schedule of benefits. The procedure for claimants has remained stable for several years. Victims must report the crime to the police within forty-eight hours after the event and must file the compensation claim within 180 days, although the board can extend this time. A claim form is submitted with supporting materials, such as medical reports, to the secretary of the board, who checks for compliance with the statute. Claims are then docketed and investigated for accuracy. When hearings are deemed necessary they are held before a single commissioner, who takes evidence presented under oath, but are not bound by the rules of a court. If the decision of the commissioner is not accepted by the claimant, he can request a hearing by the full board. All decisions are sent to the attorney general and secretary of the Department of Public Safety and Correctional Services, who can appeal a decision as improper to the appropriate court. Awards are final if there is no appeal.[34]

The compensation program, which also covers good samaritans injured or killed attempting to prevent a crime or apprehend a criminal, is limited to those who meet the hardship test. Certain assets are excluded from financial consideration: homestead, furnishings, personal effects, tools of a trade, automobile, and savings equal to the claimant's annual net income.[35]

Rather than allow judges to fine criminals to support the victim-compensation program, which has been ineffective wherever tried, Maryland law requires the imposition of $5 in court costs on all persons convicted of a crime in the state. In 1976, collecting over $130,000, this assessment paid for about 8 percent of the awards.[36] Given the reluctance of judges to fine criminals to support compensation funds, mandatory fines may be required if there is a policy goal of support by the criminals.

Hawaii. Hawaii was the first state to offer payments to crime victims for pain and suffering. Its program passed the legislature in 1967 and became operational in 1968. Besides making payments up to a maximum of $10,000 to crime victims (with no hardship test), the program compensates good samaritans "who suffer personal injury or property damage in the course of preventing a crime or apprehending a criminal."[37]

As in New York, attorneys' fees are paid out of the award and only about a fifth of the claimants are represented by lawyers. Fees are not allowed to exceed 15 percent of any award over $1,000.[38] Attorneys are unlikely to become wealthy filing compensation claims, and the executive secretary of the Criminal Injuries Compensation Commission reports that even when laywers do file the claim, the commission does most of the work.[39]

About one-quarter of a million dollars was awarded to crime victims in 1975 and in 1976. The awards averaged nearly $1,500 in those years, of which almost 40 percent was in payment for pain and suffering, which especially benefited rape victims. In 1976 only 4 of the 162 awards made were to good samaritans. Unlike most states, the program in Hawaii has remained quite stable in size since 1970, when more was given in compensation than in 1976.[40]

Massachusetts. Since July 1, 1969, Massachusetts courts have been empowered to hear claims for compensation submitted by victims of crime. The courts can award up to $10,000.

No compensation shall be paid unless the claimant has incurred an out-of-pocket loss of at least one hundred dollars or has lost two continuous weeks of earnings or support. Out-of-pocket loss shall mean unreimbursed expenses or indebtedness reasonably incurred for medical care or other services necessary as a result of the injury upon which such claim is granted. One hundred dollars shall be deducted from any award under this chapter.[41]

After a claim is filed with the district court, the clerk notifies the attorney general, who investigates the claim. The attorney general may then present relevant evidence at the hearing, at which the claimant may be represented by an attorney. The court determines attorneys' fees, which are paid out of the award and are not to exceed 15 percent of the award.[42]

This program, which is funded entirely by the legislature, has been unique in procedure until quite recently. It has grown gradually but has remained quite small, perhaps because there is not an independent agency to direct the program. In the fiscal years covering 1973 to 1976 approximately $2.1 million was awarded to less than 600 claimants, for an average award of about $3,600.[43]

Nevada. "Unfortunately, budgetary restraints and apprehensions have motivated the Nevada legislature from funding compensation to innocent victims of criminal activity."[44] Alone among the fifty states, Nevada provides a

compensation program only for good-samaritan victims of criminal acts. Passed in 1969 and making its first award in 1970, the program has remained very small. Four awards were made in 1971, two in 1974, and seven in 1975, averaging almost $4,000 per award.

A deputy attorney general hears the claims, which are investigated and documented as in the case of victim-compensation programs in other states. Attorneys' fees, which are not to exceed 10 percent of the award, are set by the state board of examiners, and are paid out of the award, which is also determined by the board. Compensation for medical expenses and loss of earning or support incurred by the intervenor or his (her) dependents cannot exceed the $5,000 maximum, which is frequently paid. Funeral expenses up to $1,000 for a good samaritan will also be paid. Although this program is generally lumped in with the compensation programs of other states, it should be noted that it is very different in that it is specifically oriented "to encourage the cooperation and assistance of the public in law enforcement and to promote the public welfare," by paying individuals for some of the costs they may incur attempting to prevent a crime or assist a police officer.[45]

In 1975 the act was amended to allow counties to provide up to $1,000 each for medical care and psychological treatment of rape victims. Counties must fund such assistance.[46]

New Jersey. Effective November 1, 1971, New Jersey became the first large state to institute a "standard" victim-compensation program without a financial-hardship test. Like other programs, the Violent Crimes Compensation Board will make lump-sum payments to cover medical expenses and lost income, protracted payments to individuals incapacitated for an extended period of time, and provide death benefits for the dependents of a deceased victim, up to a $10,000 maximum.[47] In addition to the compensation the board awards attorneys' fees, which may not exceed a rate of $40 per hour or 15 percent of the award, whichever is less.[48]

The New Jersey program has suffered from a "fiscal plight," because the board is "grossly underfunded," according to the chairman.[49] As of June 30, 1977, there was a backlog of 2,300 cases, approximately 60 percent of which were expected to qualify for awards averaging $3,500, for a total of almost $5 million in compensation. The budget for the fiscal year beginning July 1, 1977, was only $1.2 million, which was clearly insufficient to clear the backlog, let alone meet the demands of the new year. The fiscal 1977 budget was expected to be spent in the following manner: 14 percent for administration, 60 percent paid directly to victims, 35 percent paid to hospitals and physicians (on behalf of victims), and 5 percent for lawyers.[50]

Due to a shortage of state funds to cover the claims made by victims, the board has discontinued a publicity campaign it had in the past to make victims aware of the existence of the program.[51] Officials from New Jersey, like those

from other states with compensation programs, have lobbied for passage of the federal subsidy to state compensation programs. In congressional testimony in 1976, the attorney general of New Jersey claimed that, under the existing structure of the New Jersey program, compensation to victims of *reported* crime in 1975 could have reached $56.7 million, if those victims had exercised their rights.[52] The figure would be higher if New Jersey adopted a $50,000 maximum payment, which was under consideration because of the many victims who suffer losses greater than $10,000.[53] Other amendments to the compensation plan which have been introduced in the New Jersey legislature include: reduction of the minimum payment from $100 to $50, the expansion of coverage to include property loss, a requirement that all police officers notify all victims of the existence of the compensation program, and the elimination of certain requirements and procedures for rape victims.[54]

Alaska. If every state spent as much per capita on victim compensation as Alaska does, about $200 million would have been spent during fiscal year 1975-76. That year, Alaska made sixty-eight awards averaging about $4,000 each, from a total budget of one-third of a million dollars.[55]

The program has grown quite rapidly since its inauguration in March 1973. The original legislation was amended in 1975 to expand the program. Now the maximum award per victim per incident is $25,000, except in death cases, when dependents may be eligible for $40,000. The Violent Crimes Compensation Board may make emergency awards to victims up to $1,500. It pays attorneys' fees in addition to awards. The fees may not exceed 25 percent of the first $1,000 awarded, 15 percent of the next $9,000 awarded, and 7.5 percent of all compensation over $10,000. The board must consider the financial need of the victim, but, in case of death, may disregard life-insurance proceeds received by survivors. To help inform citizens of their rights, the state requires every hospital to display posters in prominent locations which explain the provisions of the program, and requires law-enforcement agencies to inform victims or their survivors of the compensation by the state.[56]

Illinois. The second state to operate a compensation program through existing courts, the Illinois Crime Victims Compensation Act became effective October 1, 1973. Victims or their survivors file a notice of intent to file a claim with the attorney general. A detailed claim must be filed with the Court of Claims within two years of the crime. The court, which has three judges and eight commissioners, adjudicates the claim, ordering the state to pay up to $10,000 to the successful claimant, to cover medical expenses and lost wages or support, less a $200 deductible. Claimants must pay their attorneys out of the award received, under the supervision of the court.[57]

Compensation claims constitute about one-half of the workload of the

Court of Claims now, so that the court has become somewhat burdened.[58] Like New Jersey, the compensation fund has been inadequate, creating a backlog of claims. Through 1975 the court had closed 508 claims, granting an average of $3,100 to 352 successful claimants. There were 1,623 claims waiting to be heard at the end of 1975.[59] The director of the Crime Victims Compensation Division of the office of the attorney general of Illinois reported that the attorney general intended to sue criminals for contribution to the compensation program.[60]

Washington. Striking a new path in victim compensation, the state of Washington expanded its workmen's-compensation program to cover crime victims. The Crime Victims Compensation Division was established within the Department of Labor and Industries effective July 1, 1974, but claims could be made for crimes which occurred beginning January 1, 1972.

Since the workmen's-compensation schedule was adopted, there is no minimum or maximum claim level. All medical expenses related to the victimization not covered by other sources are paid by the program. In cases of death the surviving spouse and dependents receive a pension, a worker fully disabled by a crime receives a pension for life, and a worker who loses time from work is paid at the pension rate for the lost time. The pension rate (as of 1972) runs from 60 percent of the worker's wage per month for an unmarried worker (with a guaranteed minimum payment of $185 per month) up to 75 percent of the worker's wage for a married worker with five or more children (with a minimum payment of $352 per month). The maximum amount of any monthly payment is 75 percent of the state's average wage at the time of injury. Payments to a surviving spouse cease upon remarriage, but surviving children continue to receive payments, until age eighteen (age twenty-one if enrolled in school), equal to the portion of the pension provided because of the existence of the children. Surviving spouses also receive up to $800 for funeral expenses. Survivors of an unemployed victim receive lump-sum payments in lieu of a pension: $7,500 to the spouse, $2,500 to each child (up to five children). Permanent partial disabilities are awarded payments estimated to be in line with the extent of the disability. Many injuries are covered by a list of specific payments: loss of one leg or one arm, $18,000; loss of foot, $12,600; loss of index finger, $3,240; loss of one eye, $7,200; loss of hearing in both ears, $14,400; etc.[61] Many injuries combine the above benefits, such as a lump-sum payment for loss of limb, coverage of related medical expenses, and a pension payment for work time lost.

Claims submitted are investigated, but the procedure is nonadversary unless a claimant is dissatisfied with the award given and appeals to the Board of Appeals, which happens in less than 10 percent of the cases.[62] As in other states with compensation, the victim still has the right to sue the criminal for

damages, but recovery means that the victim must repay the state.[63] Hence, there would seem to be little incentive to sue a criminal, as the victim would have to bear the cost of the suit and would emerge wealthier only if the criminal could afford to pay a judgment larger than the payment received by the victim from the state. As of mid-1976, about $1.2 million had been paid in benefits. Payments under this system were averaging less than $1,000 (not counting the value of pensions), considerably less than in the states with "traditional" compensation programs.[64]

Minnesota. Establishing a program similar to those adopted in most states at that time, Minnesota created the Crime Victims Reparations Board effective July 1, 1974. The program has been kept quite small. In fiscal 1975-76 its budget was $300,000 less than Alaska's. After a $100 deductible, payments can rise to the maximum of $10,000 for losses similar to those compensated by other states' programs. There is no provision for attorneys' fees, but the board does guard against excessive fees charged the claimants.[65]

Minnesota is among the minority of states which allow compensation for expenses incurred in treating mental or nervous shock. As in tort law this concept has varying interpretations, but in this case it does appear to cover purely mental afflictions.[66] At the end of two full years of operations the board had granted 269 claims averaging over $1,200.[67]

Delaware. Effective the beginning of 1975, the Delaware program compensating crime victims has a few distinguishing characteristics: the deductible is $25 (the maximum payment is $10,000), there can be compensation for "extreme mental suffering," the Violent Crimes Compensation Board pays attorneys' fees in addition to awards (fee not to exceed $1,000 or 15 percent of the award), and there is a victim-compensation fund comprised of mandatory 10 percent additional penalties levied on every fine assessed to any criminal defendant, whether or not the fine is suspended.[68]

North Dakota. Placing its Crime Victims Reparations program within its Workmen's Compensation Bureau like the state of Washington, adopting the forms used by the program in Minnesota, and implementing the Uniform Crime Victims Reparations Act prepared by the National Conference of Commissioners on Uniform State Laws, North Dakota attempted to use the best features of existing programs.[69] Although jurisdiction is within the Workmen's Compensation Bureau, and uses many of its procedures, the compensation program is more of the standard variety.

A small state with little crime, after a year and a half of operations, which began July 1, 1975, only $91,000 had been spent in North Dakota. There were twenty-six awards granted during that time, averaging about $3,000 each.[70] There is no financial-hardship test, awards range from $100 to $25,000, pain

and suffering is not compensable, but attorneys' fees are paid by the board, even if the claim is unsuccessful, so long as it is not "frivolous."[71] Despite this generous treatment of attorneys, little is expected to be paid to them based on the state's experience with workmen's compensation. In fiscal 1974-75, attorneys' fees represented 0.29 percent of the $7.7 million paid in workmen's-compensation benefits.[72]

Kentucky. Instituting a "typical" compensation program on June 19, 1976, Kentucky pays awards ranging from $100 to $15,000 only in case of financial hardship. Attorneys' fees are determined by the Crime Victims Compensation Board and are paid out of the award, but not exceeding 15 percent of the award. Weekly support payments for time lost from work cannot exceed $150. After a little more than a year of operations, the board had paid thirty-five awards averaging $2,600.[73]

Ohio. Like Illinois, Ohio placed its victim-compensation program within the jurisdiction of its Court of Claims. Claims are investigated by the attorney general's office, decisions are made by the commissioners of the Court of Claims, and appeals are decided by the judges of the court. Victimizations suffered after January 3, 1976, are covered, but claims could not be filed before December 28, 1976. The maximum award is $50,000. The awards are to be covered in part by the Reparations Rotary Fund, which will receive $3 from every person convicted of any offense in the state of Ohio, except for nonmoving traffic violations. There is no financial-hardship test or provision for attorneys' fees.[74]

Wisconsin. Effective the first of 1977, victims who meet a financial-hardship test are eligible for compensation to cover between $200 and $10,000 in costs due to crime. The Crime Victim Compensation Bureau is a part of the Department of Industry, Labor and Human Relations. It conducts investigations similar to those conducted for workmen's-compensation cases, but provides standard victim-compensation coverage. Appeals are heard by the three-member commission of the department. Attorneys may receive a fee no larger than 20 percent of the award and are paid out of the award.[75] After six months of operation twenty-two claims had been paid an average of $2,300, which did not include further medical costs which were to be covered in some cases.[76]

Pennsylvania. Establishing the Crime Victim's Compensation Board within the Department of Justice, effective March 28, 1977, Pennsylvania implemented a "typical" compensation plan. There is no hardship test. Victims are eligible for payments ranging from $100 to $25,000 maximum, but no more than $10,000 for lost wages or support, except in the case of good samaritans, who may receive up to $15,000. Decisions require approval by at least two of the three

board members, who can also approve attorneys' fees, not to exceed 15 percent of the award, in addition to the award.[77]

Virginia. The first state to attempt to fund a compensation program solely by use of a Criminal Injuries Compensation Fund, after July 1, 1976, most convictions in Virginia require the imposition of a $10 fine in addition to any other punishment. Those fines are intended to be the only source available to pay compensation awards granted after July 1, 1977, when the compensation program was effected. Only victims who meet the financial-hardship test will be able to win awards under this program, which is administered by the Industrial Commission. Awards for loss of earnings due to disability are based upon the workmen's-compensation schedule. Other costs incurred by victims of their survivors are subject to a $100 deductible and may not exceed $10,000. There is no provision for attorneys' fees.[78]

Michigan. Effective October 1, 1977, the Crime Victims Compensation Board of Michigan will make payments to crime victims in a "typical" compensation program. Up to $15,000 may be awarded to cover medical expenses and up to $100 a week may be paid for loss of support or earnings. The board will establish rules regarding attorneys. As in most other states, Michigan can sue convicted criminals for reimbursement of the compensation paid by the state.[79]

Florida. Adopting a program similar to the one implemented in Virginia, effective the first of 1978 Florida provides compensation for victims suffering serious financial hardship. Although the Florida Crimes Compensation Commission is within the Department of Health and Rehabilitative Services, like Virginia it is to apply workmen's-compensation benefits to cover lost wages. Other losses are covered up to $10,000. Attorneys' fees are to be based upon the amount of work done, paid by the commission whether or not there is an award given, unless the claim is frivolous. Adopting the most ambitious financing scheme of any state, but not relying upon it entirely, the Florida statute provides that any person who pleads guilty or *nolo contendere* or is convicted of any felony or misdemeanor must pay $10 in addition to any other punishment, unless the fine would cause severe financial hardship. This money is to be paid into the Crimes Compensation Trust Fund, which will be supplemented by a 5 percent surcharge on all fines, civil penalties, and forfeitures levied against individuals under any statute or ordinance. When an individual is convicted of, or pleads guilty or *nolo contendere* to, any felony or misdemeanor which resulted in the injury or death of another person, the court, taking into account the financial position of the defendant, may fine him up to $10,000 in addition to any other punishment, to be paid into the trust fund.[80] In addition, courts may make repayment of compensation to the trust fund a condition of parole or probation.[81]

Tennessee. Placing its victim-compensation program entirely within its court system, Tennessee intends to finance its compensation by $20 fines collected from every person convicted of a crime, in addition to other punishment. The Criminal Injuries Compensation Fund is also to receive money from individuals placed on parole or probation, who can be required to pay up to 10 percent of their income to the fund. Circuit courts will make awards based upon claims investigated by local district attorneys. Awards up to $10,000 can be made to victims suffering at least two weeks lost from work or a $100 loss. Attorneys will receive up to 15 percent of the award granted, paid by the court in addition to the compensation. Payments for pain and suffering can be made in case of rape or sexual-deviancy crimes. A judge who convicts a criminal may not make the determination of compensation for the victim(s) of that criminal.[82]

Although funds have been collected since July 1, 1976, there can be no compensation for crimes which occurred before July 1, 1978. The first year of the fund was not very successful. Apparently the courts were frequently failing to collect the $20 fine from defendants convicted of crimes, so, as in most jurisdictions, this method of financing may be insufficient to cover the claims for victim compensation.[83]

Other States. Rhode Island enacted a victim-compensation plan in 1972 which would pay up to $25,000 to victims. Pain and suffering would be compensable, as would all other costs incurred by victims. Attorneys would be paid by the special court which would decide cases. There is also to be an indemnity fund created from 20 percent of the money paid in fines and penalties from all criminal charges. "This act shall take effect thirty (30) days following the enactment of federal legislation entitled "The victims of crime act.""[84] Since the federal subsidy has not been approved, there is no active program in Rhode Island.

In 1976 the Louisiana legislature repealed the victim-compensation statute it had passed several years before, but had never funded.[85] Apparently, like Rhode Island, Louisiana was awaiting federal funding, but may have been stimulated to repeal the legislation by a court decision that the state had to process claims for compensation even though it did not have to pay compensation.[86]

The Virgin Islands passed a compensation program in 1968. It pays up to $10,000 in awards, including up to $500 for pain and suffering. The program is operated by the Virgin Islands Crime Victim Compensation Commission.[87]

Occasionally, Texas is cited as having a very limited form of compensation. Actually the law simply states that if a law-enforcement agency in Texas wants a medical examination to provide evidence in a rape case, that agency must pay for the examination.[88]

Georgia: Something Different. Since 1967 it has been possible for the Claims Advisory Board to suggest compensation up to $5,000 for good samaritans.[89] However, every claim must be approved by the legislature, so that the statute has been used very little. However, rather than moving to implement compensation for crime victims, Georgia is attempting to establish an offender-restitution program.[90]

As noted before, restitution is payment from the criminal to the victim, not payment from taxpayers to the victim, as in the case of compensation. The restitution program was initially funded by the Law Enforcement Assistance Administration (LEAA). Displaying acceptance of the program, the Georgia legislature began full state funding of the program in fiscal year 1977. A variation of the program, which is operated by the Department of Offender Rehabilitation, is currently funded by the LEAA.

Restitution is difficult because many offenders do not have sufficient resources to pay restitution. The prison system is not designed to enable prisoners to work productively, as is discussed in Appendix A, so while incarcerated they cannot earn money to pay their victims. The Georgia program is designed to counter these problems by diverting some offenders (mostly felons) to the restitution program in lieu of imprisonment. Unsatisfactory participation by an offender can result in revocation of his parole or probation status, placing him in prison.

Restitution centers operate in four cities, full time, handling 25 to 33 offenders each, for a total capability of 120. Offenders live at the centers, but are allowed periodic home visits. The staff of each center is comprised of professionals, VISTA volunteers, student interns, and citizen volunteers. The offender is assisted in obtaining employment, so that he can earn money to be able to pay restitution. Offenders' paychecks are turned over to the center, which devises a budget plan for each person. It is hoped that this will enable offenders to support their families, so they are not reduced to welfare status, while paying the debt owed the victim.

In each case a judge determines how much restitution must be paid by an offender. Most offenders are allowed to leave the centers and return home once they have demonstrated stability and responsibility on the job and with respect to the debt owed. Probationers may also be required to perform some community service in lieu of or in addition to financial restitution. This includes such projects as working in public hospitals, repairing the homes of aged pensioners, working with juvenile offenders, and cleaning up the community.

Participation by the victim is usually minimal. Generally, the victim is sent a letter explaining the program and a restitution payment. Occasionally, it has been arranged for the offender to repay the victim in a controlled face-to-face situation. Although most victims do not care for such meetings, they have been quite successful when used.

From July 1975 through December 1976, offenders paid $126,987 to

victims, $241,690 in state and federal taxes, $342,937 to the state for room and board, $139,513 to support their families, spent $431,704 on living expenses, saved $84,156, and contributed over 4,000 hours of public service restitution work.[91] Although the program appears to be cheaper than imprisonment, its cost-effectiveness is not fully determined. However, its operators are optimistic and the program appears to have won acceptance by the legislature. The program can be considered as a substitute for or complement to some compensation and the traditional prison-parole-probation system of dealing with some offenders.

Federal Compensation

Various victim-assistance programs throughout the United States are funded by $49.3 million in grants from the LEAA. In 1977 there were at least 114 of these programs, in addition to the state programs, most of which were federally funded. The LEAA has been supporting these experiments since 1973. These programs provide a number of different services. Some provide physical assistance for victims, others help victims sue for restitution or apply for welfare benefits, and some help victims prepare for testimony against assailants.[92] Most of these programs could disappear if federal assistance for state compensation programs is forthcoming.

Former Senator Ralph Yarborough of Texas introduced the first federal "Victims of Crime Act" in the Congress in June 1965.[93] The bill has been reintroduced, with modifications, in every session of Congress since then. A compromise version of the bill, sponsored by Senators Mansfield and McClellan, passed the Senate in September of 1972 by a vote of 60-8, and was passed again in 1973 by the Senate.[94] Some form of federal legislation to provide states with funds for compensation "now stands a fair chance in Congress after three years of rejection."[95]

Some proposals would establish a Violent Crimes Compensation Board as an independent agency within the Justice Department.[96] It would be composed of three members, appointed by the president with the approval of Congress. One board member would be designated chairman. His qualifications would be that he must have been a member of federal court or of the highest court of a state for at least eight years. No board member would be allowed to engage in any other business during the time of his service. Although the positions of executive secretary and general counsel are decreed, the board would have broad powers to create whatever full-time staff positions and advisory committees it believes necessary to execute its functions.

The board would have full power of subpoena and operate much as a court does, except that it could admit anything as evidence deemed appropriate in the opinion of the board members. Hearings could be held in private

when the interests of the victims would be best served in that manner, or when the criminal has not been tried, so as not to bias the judicial proceedings. All attorneys who appear before the board in connection with any case could file for and collect their fees from the board.

After deducting any private insurance payments received, the board would be authorized to make payments of not less than $100 in any one case, to be paid in lump sum or on a periodic basis. Victims in federal jurisdictions would be entitled to be compensated for medical expenses, loss of earnings, and other pecuniary losses up to $50,000. Good samaritans would be entitled to collect for property losses, though there would be no maximum limit in these cases. These payments would apply to injuries sustained as a result of any proven criminal act.

A Criminal Victim Indemnity Fund would be established to help pay for the awards. All federal courts would take into consideration the financial condition of convicted felons, who have caused personal injury, property loss, or death, and order those persons to pay fines of not more than $10,000, in addition to any other penalty. All other funds would come through the Department of Justice budget.

The Violent Crimes Compensation Board would sit on all cases which arise in federal jurisdictions, such as the District of Columbia and Puerto Rico, and would be authorized to pay for 50 to 75 percent (different bills offered different percents) of the costs of state operated programs which meet the standards set by the Board. Funds would be administered through the Department of Justice.

The bill reported by the House Committee on the Judiciary in 1977 (H.R. 7010) abandoned the idea of a federal compensation program.[97] Instead, the federal government would pay the states for 100 percent of the compensation granted by state programs to victims of crime subject to exclusive federal jurisdiction, and pay 50 percent of the costs of the state compensation programs.

By the terms of H.R. 7010, the attorney general would appoint a nine-member Advisory Committee on Victims of Crime, seven of whom would be officials of states with compensation programs. This advisory committee would help the attorney general determine how much assistance to give states which have compensation programs. Forty million dollars is provided for the fiscal year ending September 30, 1978, $50 million for the following year, and $60 million for the next fiscal year.

Subject to certain guidelines, which are similar to the rules of existing compensation programs, states would be paid for 50 percent of the costs of compensation, except for: awards for pain and suffering, for property loss, or for more than $50,000; administrative costs; awards covering costs of less than $100; awards for lost earnings of more than $200 per week; or awards to any victim who failed to notify the policy of the crime within seventy-two hours or who failed to file a claim within one year of the crime.[98]

Given the federal subsidization of state compensation programs, it is likely that most states would implement such programs, and compensation would be available nationwide. Existing programs in over twenty states, which cover about 60 percent of the nation's population, may have to be slightly modified to meet federal standards for subsidization.

Notes

1. James E. Culhane, "California Enacts Legislation to Aid Victims of Criminal Violence," *Stanford Law Review* 43 (November 1965), p. 266.

2. State Board of Control, "Indemnification of Private Citizens," data part of annual report. Correspondence from State Board of Control, Sacramento, California, to author, November 1974.

3. Culhane, "California Enacts Legislation," pp. 268-69.

4. *California Welfare and Institutions Code,* 11211 (1966), cited in Edelhertz and Geis, *Public Compensation*, p. 81.

5. William Shank, "Aid to Victims of Violent Crimes in California," *Southern California Law Review* 43 (1970), p. 86.

6. Herbert Edelhertz and Gilbert Geis, "California's New Crime Victim Compensation Statute," *San Diego Law Review* 11 (1974), pp. 886-87.

7. Shank, "Aid to Victims in California," p. 87.

8. Edelhertz and Geis, *Public Compensation,* p. 83.

9. Shank, "Aid to Victims in California," pp. 89-91.

10. *Senate Bill No. 149,* Chapter 1144, October 2, 1973, State of California.

11. Edelhertz and Geis, "California's New Statute," p. 885.

12. Ibid., pp. 888-89.

13. State Board of Control, "Indemnification of Private Citizens," Sections 13959, et seq., 13970 et seq., Government Code. Correspondence of June 1977 from State Board of Control, Sacramento, California, to author.

14. U.S., House, Committee on the Judiciary, *Crime Victim Compensation,* Hearings, 94th Cong., 1975 and 1976, serial no. 39, p. 505.

15. Herbert Edelhertz et al., "Part I – Public Compensation of Victims of Crime: A Survey of the New York Experience," *Criminal Law Bulletin* 9 (January 1973), pp. 8-11. Collins' widow received an annuity worth $4,420.26.

16. Ibid., pp. 14-27.

17. *New York Times,* March 15, 1973, p. 45.

18. Crime Victims Compensation Board, *Seventh Annual Report,* State of New York, Legislative Document (1974), no. 94, pp. 6-7.

19. Herbert Edelhertz et al., "Part II – Public Compensation of Victims

of Crime: A Survey of the New York Experience," *Criminal Law Bulletin* 9 (March 1973), p. 110.

20. Michael J. Novack, "Crime Victim Compensation: The New York Solution," *Albany Law Review* 35 (1971), pp. 725-27.

21. U.S., House, *Crime Victim Compensation,* pp. 302-305.

22. Edlehertz et al., "Part II — Public Compensation," pp. 108–109.

23. Edelhertz et al., "Part I — Public Compensation," pp. 30-31.

24. Crime Victims Compensation Board, *1975 Annual Report,* State of New York (1976), p. 8.

25. Ibid., pp. 8-12.

26. Ibid., p. 19.

27. U.S., House, *Crime Victim Compensation,* p. 1274.

28. Ibid., pp. 1273-74.

29. Crime Victims Compensation Board, *1975 Annual Report,* p. 23.

30. Crime Victims Compensation Board, *Seventh Annual Report,* p. 12.

31. Criminal Injuries Compensation Board, *Seventh Annual Report,* State of Maryland, 1976, pp. 3, 5.

32. U.S., House, *Crime Victim Compensation,* p. 28.

33. Ibid., p. 25.

34. Criminal Injuries Compensation Board, *Seventh Annual Report,* pp. 1-5.

35. Note, "Criminal Victim Compensation in Maryland," *Maryland Law Review* 30 (Summer 1970), pp. 280-82.

36. Criminal Injuries Compensation Board, *Seventh Annual Report,* p. 5.

37. Criminal Injuries Compensation Commission, *Ninth Annual Report,* State of Hawaii, 1976, p. 1.

38. *Hawaii Revised Statutes,* § 351-16 (1967).

39. U.S., House, *Crime Victim Compensation,* p. 425.

40. Criminal Injuries Compensation Commission, *Ninth Annual Report,* Appendix D.

41. *Massachusetts General Laws,* ch. 258A, § 5 (1968).

42. Ibid., § 4.

43. Based on statistics provided by the Department of the Attorney General, Commonwealth of Massachusetts, in correspondence with author, October 1974 and July 1977.

44. Communication from Deputy Attorney General of Nevada to author, June 1977.

45. *Nevada Revised Statutes* ch. 217 (1969).

46. Ibid., ch. 217, § § 280-350 (1975).

47. Violent Crimes Compensation Board, *First Annual Report,* State of New Jersey, 1973, pp. 1-4.

48. Violent Crimes Compensation Board, *Annual Report — Calendar Year 1975,* State of New Jersey, p. 3.

49. Correspondence of author with Chairman, Violent Crimes Compensation Board, State of New Jersey, July 1977.

50. Ibid.

51. Violent Crimes Compensation Board, *Annual Report—1975*, p.1.

52. U.S., House, *Crime Victim Compensation*, p. 281.

53. Ibid., p. 280.

54. Violent Crimes Compensation Board, *Annual Report—1975*, p. 7.

55. Violent Crimes Compensation Board, *Third Annual Report*, State of Alaska, 1976, pp. 7-8.

56. *Alaska Statutes*, § § 18.67.010-.180 (1975).

57. U.S., House, *Crime Victim Compensation*, pp. 110-12.

58. Ibid., p. 115.

59. Clerk, Illinois Court of Claims, "Illinois Crime Victims Compensation Act, October 1, 1973-December 31, 1975."

60. U.S., House, *Crime Victim Compensation*, pp. 145–46.

61. *Revised Code of Washington* Title 51 (1973).

62. U.S., House, *Crime Victim Compensation*, p. 402.

63. *Revised Code of Washington*, ch. 7.68.050 (1973).

64. Crime Victim Compensation Division, *First Report*, Department of Labor and Industries, State of Washington, October 1, 1976, pp. 4-11.

65. Crime Victims Reparations Board, *First Biennial Report*, State of Minnesota, 1976, pp. 1-3.

66. Note, "The Minnesota Crime Victims Reparations Act: A Preliminary Analysis," *William Mitchell Law Review* 2 (1976), pp. 216-18.

67. Statistics provided to author by Minnesota Crime Victims Reparations Board, correspondence of July 1977.

68. *Delaware Code Annotated*, title 11, ch. 90 (Cum. Supp. 1976).

69. Richard J. Gross, "Crime Victim Compensation in North Dakota: A Year of Trial and Error," *North Dakota Law Review* 53 (1976), pp. 14-17.

70. Statistics provided to author by Crime Victims Reparations Office, North Dakota, correspondence of July 1977.

71. Gross, "Compensation in North Dakota," pp. 18, 30.

72. Ibid., p. 31.

73. Information provided to author by Kentucky Crime Victims Compensation Board, correspondence of August 1977. See *Kentucky Revised Statutes*, ch. 346.

74. *Ohio Revised Code*, § § 2743.0.-.72 (1976).

75. *Wisconsin Statutes*, ch. 949 (1976).

76. Statistics provided to author by Crime Victim Compensation Bureau of Wisconsin, correspondence of July 1977.

77. *Pennsylvania Statutes*, § 180-7 et seq. (West Supp. 1977).

78. *Code of Virginia*, § § 19.2-368.1-.18 (1977).

79. *Michigan Comp. Laws Ann.*, § § 18.351-.368 (West Supp. 1977).

80. This provision may be, as in most jurisdictions where tried, relatively useless. However, in the judgment of the author, Florida judges appear to be more "conservative," and may, therefore, be more disposed to make use of such provisions, especially because many judicial positions are elected in Florida.

81. *Florida Statutes,* §§ 897.01-.25, .03; 142.01, .03; 775.083; 947.18; 948.03.

82. *Tennessee Code Annotated,* §§ 23-3501 et seq., 40-3207; *Public Acts of 1977,* ch. 427 (Tennessee).

83. Letter from Attorney for the Board of Claims, State of Tennessee, to author, July 1977.

84. *Rhode Island General Laws Annotated,* ch. 24-12 (Supp. 1975).

85. *Louisiana Statutes Annotated,* §§ 46.1801-1821 (West Supp. 1977).

86. *Wolf v. State,* App. 1975, 325 So.2d 342.

87. *Virgin Islands Code,* §§ 151-177 (1976).

88. *Texas Civil Statutes,* art. 4474m (1976).

89. *Code of Georgia Annotated,* §§ 47-518–524 (1974).

90. The discussion of the restitution program is drawn entirely from: Bill Read, Restitution Program Coordinator, *Offender Restitution Programs in Georgia,* Georgia Department of Offender Rehabilitation, Atlanta, Georgia, 1977.

91. Ibid., pp. 7-8.

92. "Victims of Crime Get Counseling, Other Aid in Many Areas of U.S.," *Wall Street Journal,* August 22, 1977, p. 1.

93. Ralph W. Yarborough, "The Battle for a Federal Violent Crimes Compensation Act; The Genesis of S.9," *Southern California Law Review* 43 (1970), pp. 93-106.

94. "Votes in Congress," *New York Times,* September 23, 1972, p. 25. U.S., Congress, House, *Victims of Crime Act of 1973,* 93rd Cong., 1st sess., 1973, S. 300.

95. "Victims of Crime," *Wall Street Journal,* August 22, 1977, p. 1.

96. *S.300,* 93rd Cong., 1st sess. (1973).

97. *H.R.7010,* 95th Cong., 1st sess. (1977).

98. Ibid., § 5.

4

Public Choice
Considerations of
Victim Compensation

The proposed federal program to assist victims of crimes presents an interesting opportunity for the application of some aspects of the theory of public choice developed in recent years. In particular, there is a significant opportunity for application of the emerging theory of bureaucracy. This chapter explores why the victim-compensation bill has emerged, why it should pass Congress, how much it is apt to cost in operation, who the major beneficiaries would be, and how the government officials running the programs could be expected to behave in pressing for expansion.

Potential Costs of a Compensation Program

In a crude calculation of the possible cost of national victim compensation, Duane G. Harris estimated that in 1970 public victim compensation would have cost over $1 billion.[1] Harris based his estimate on the assumption that 700,000 victims of violent crimes (the estimated number in 1970) would all receive compensation payments averaging about $1,500 each, which was comparable to workmen's-compensation payments in New York and Pennsylvania. Extrapolating this figure to 1975, Harris's method of estimation would yield an annual cost of about $3.5 billion.[2]

A 1972 staff study by the Program and Management Evaluation Division of the Office of Operations Support of the Law Enforcement Assistance Administration (LEAA) estimated that, if compensation programs were implemented in every state by fiscal 1974, and if the federal program providing 75 percent subsidization of the state programs were effective, by fiscal 1979, when the program would be operational nationwide, it would cost $26,845,000. Of this, $21,084,793 would be the share of the federal government. This cost estimate took the New York and Maryland state compensation programs' cost figures for the early 1970s and extrapolated the numbers to the rest of the country. It accounted for the lower crime rates in other states and the higher maximum payment allowed by the federal plan. The LEAA believed this estimate was superior to another projection which simply extrapolated the New York and Maryland programs nationally, yielding a total cost estimate of $34,200,000 for fiscal 1976.[3] However, this latter figure was accepted as most appropriate by the congressional sponsors of the victim-compensation bill: Hence the $40 million appropriation provided by H.R. 7010 for the fiscal year ending in 1978.

A cost estimate prepared by the Congressional Budget Office (CBO) in 1977, based upon H.R. 7010, which provides a 50 percent subsidy for state programs, estimated that in fiscal 1978 only $22 million of the $40 million appropriated by the bill would be spent.[4] In 1979 only $29 million of the $50 million appropriated would be spent, and in 1980 only $35 million of the $60 million appropriated would be spent.

The Harris estimate is very crude and may be rejected on the grounds that some of its assumptions are inappropriate. In particular, the condition that all victims would receive compensation is incorrect, at least for the near future. On the other hand, the LEAA and CBO estimates seem designed primarily to stimulate support for the program, which would benefit the Department of Justice and is supported by the majority, which controls the CBO. Bureaus often understate the estimated cost of new programs so that they are more appealing to legislators. In any case, that estimate is based on assumptions of dubious validity, as will be discussed.

It is true that an accurate estimate is difficult. One based on conservative assumptions is made below, utilizing some limitations assumed by bureaucrats involved with compensation programs. Since bureaucrats have incentives to understate the likely costs of new programs, this estimate may be suspected to be on the low side.

An analysis prepared for the State Senate of Washington of the victim-compensation bill that was passed and implemented there in 1973 contains esimates of the future cost of the program. The estimates were based primarily on the experience of the state of Maryland, which has had a compensation program for a relatively long time and, as a state, is similar to Washington in size and in amount of crime. The Maryland program is also the closest to the federal proposal in coverage. Based on previous program performance in Maryland, both states estimated that 5.8 percent of all victims of violent crimes would receive compensation in fiscal 1975.[5]

An estimate of the number of victims of violent crimes resulting in injury is given in table 4-1, using statistics provided by the comprehensive victimization survey taken by the LEAA for 1975. The estimates of criminal victimization provided by the LEAA surveys are used here rather than the FBI's *Uniform Crime Reports,* which have been the traditional source of estimates of victimization. The LEAA surveys have revealed that most crimes are not reported to the police. This estimate excludes some crimes which potentially would also be compensated, such as murder, arson, and crimes inflicted on persons under twelve years of age. It also excludes millions of crimes "when the extent of the injury was minor (e.g., bruises, black eyes, cuts, scratches, swelling) or is undetermined but requiring less than 2 days of hospitalization."[6]

Assuming that only 5.8 percent of the crimes with injury were compensated, there would have been 100,000 awards nationally in 1975. The average compensation award in 1975 in several states with high maximum payments,

Table 4-1

Victimization Rate per 1,000 Population Age 12 and Over for Incidents Resulting in Injury[a]

Crime	1975 Rate	Total Number
Rape and attempted rape	0.9	150,100
Robbery with injury	2.1	350,100
Aggravated assault with injury	3.3	550,200
Simple assault with injury	4.1	683,600
Total		1,734,000

Source: U.S., National Criminal Justice Information and Statistics Service, *Criminal Victimization in the United States: A Comparison of the 1974 and 1975 Findings,* National Crime Panel Survey Report, no. SD–NCP–NS (Washington, D.C.: U.S.G.P.O., 1977), p. 9.

[a]Population age 12 and over was 166.7 million. Injury is defined as "serious injury (e.g., broken bones, loss of teeth, internal injuries, loss of consciousness) or in undetermined injury requiring 2 or more days of hospitalization."

like Maryland, was about $4,000. The $4,000 figure is used here because of the $50,000 maximum payment allowed by the federal government and because of the experiences of several states.

Multiplying these figures yields a total compensation bill of $400 million nationally for 1975. This amount ignores administrative costs, which would add at least another 10 percent to this total. Considering the crime rate and the fact that hospitalization costs are increasing, an estimate of a $.5 billion annual outlay for the late 1970s would not seem out of order, based on the assumptions made here. This estimate does not account for the expenditure impact of federal subsidization, which will be discussed later.[7]

Support for a cost estimate far in excess of those estimated by the LEAA and CBO is provided by several independent sources. It was estimated that in 1973 in New York City 3.2 percent of the victims of crime would have been eligible for compensation. Assuming the same level of payments as used in the estimate here, this would yield a national compensation expenditure of over $200 million, with a requirement of "serious financial hardship."[8] There is no financial-hardship test in the federal subsidy, so it may be that many states would do away with that limitation, which would expand the number of eligible victims.

As noted before, the Attorney General of New Jersey estimated that compensation could reach $57.6 million per year in New Jersey, based on 1975 figures.[9] Assuming New Jersey to have a crime rate similar to the rest of the nation, expanding that estimate to a national level would yield over $1.6 billion in expenditures.

Surveys taken in 1974 and 1975 in Milwaukee County provide estimates of the numbers of victims potentially eligible for compensation.[10] Costs over $100

due to physical injury were reported by 7.2 percent of all victims. Over $100 income was lost by 10.8 percent of the victims, and 11.5 percent lost over five days' time (one work week) due to their victimization. All of these victims would meet the guidelines established by the federal subsidy. These figures are with respect to all crime victims interviewed, not just the victims of crimes producing serious injury as defined in the LEAA surveys used here. There were almost 5.5 million crimes of violence in 1975, according to the LEAA victimization survey.[11] If approximately 10 percent of these victims were eligible for compensation, as indicated by the Milwaukee sample, then over half a million crime victims could qualify for compensation. If all victims averaged compensation awards of only $1,000 each, then there would be over $.5 billion in awards.

Political Pressures

A victim-compensation program of the size just discussed would be large enough to make some difference in the financial position of numerous crime victims. The LEAA Staff Report, on the other hand, envisioned annual compensation of about $25 million. If awards average $1,000, which is below what is given currently in any state with a compensation program, only 25,000 victims, less than 2 percent of the victims of crimes with injury, would be assisted annually. A program of this magnitude simply would be insignificant and would stir little interest in any sector. In fact, numerous groups have actively supported the measure, presumably because there are incentives to do so. One can consider some of the possible motives of the supporters, noting which groups perceive benefits from passage, and why there is no organized opposition to the bill.

The American Bar Association has enthusiastically endorsed a governmental compensation program.[12] The rationale for this support is easy to discover. As proposed, most federal bills would allow all individuals who wish to file a claim for compensation to do so with or without the assistance of a lawyer. However, if one secures the services of a lawyer in pressing a claim, whether that claim is successful or not, the compensation board would pay the fees of the lawyer. A similar provision is included in the Uniform Crime Victims Reparations Act approved by the American Bar Association.[13]

In several states' victim compensation programs lawyers receive 15 percent of the award given the victim, out of the victims' payments. Applying this percentage to the estimated $.5 billion to be given in awards, lawyers might collect $75 million annually for successful claims alone. Assuming that a lawyer can operate an office for about $75,000 a year, including his salary, office help, office rental, and other expenses, the pursuit of successful claims could provide full-time employment for 1,000 lawyers.[14] In a rapidly growing profession such subsidies are welcomed; this program would not support a massive number of lawyers, but a number large enough to make action by the lobbying arm of the

profession worthwhile. Since many congressmen are lawyers, they undoubtedly see as reasonable this provision of the proposed program.

The International Association of Chiefs of Police was an early supporter of compensation for crime victims, unanimously passing a resolution in favor of adoption at the 1966 annual conference.[15] Although there is no direct assistance for policemen in the compensation legislation, it usually was joined with legislation providing federal payments for policemen and firemen killed in the line of duty. By supporting both pieces of legislation some logrolling is accomplished, although it is possible that victim compensation would be supported on its own merits.

The continual growth of crime has placed the efficiency and quality of public police services under question.[16] Most citizens who are victimized have little incentive to call the police because usually there is little the police can do for them.[17] The odds that the police will capture criminals are low, so that without some monetary reward victims will simply incur time costs by cooperating with the police.[18] This was illustrated by the Milwaukee survey of victims. One-third of the victims reported a loss of income due to entrance into the criminal-justice system.[19] Over $100 in income was lost by 6.3 percent of the victims. Almost 60 percent of the victims reported a time loss due to cooperation with the criminal-justice system.

A compensation program would have a potential two-fold beneficial effect for police bureaus. First, because some victims would be compensated, the public might be mollified that something is "being done" for the innocent victims, for whom there is general sympathy. This would relieve some of the pressure on the police to "do something" about the criminals. Second, because one must report a crime to the police to be able to apply for compensation, there would be an increase in the number of crimes reported. This added work load and perceived increase in crime would provide justification for an increase in police budgets.

The Department of Justice would benefit from the adoption of the compensation program. Because the federal program funds would be administered through the Department of Justice, the department would be expanded in size, budget, and sphere of influence. This could account for the LEAA study, which pushed for adoption of the program, claiming that the cost would be trivial. The message to the politicians is that a visible and probably popular program can be instituted at little cost. Even if the estimate is wrong, it is doubtful that any punitive action would be taken against the agency responsible for the estimate, especially years after the fact. The LEAA study employed highly suspect assumptions which severely lowered the estimated cost. Once implemented, however, the federal government would be bound by the law to pay for whatever costs the program incurred. Congressmen would be hard pressed to vote for a reduction of benefits to innocent victims of crime.

The political popularity of compensation programs is evidenced by their rapid adoption in most Anglo-Saxon jurisdictions, including over twenty American

states since 1965 (not including "Good Samaritan" statutes). Because the states would benefit significantly from the federal subsidy, and the officials running the state programs would benefit the most, there has been much lobbying by the states for enactment of the federal program.[20] Some states passed victim-compensation legislation but have been waiting to fund their programs until the federal subsidy becomes available. The compensation bill easily passed the Senate in September 1972 and again in March 1973. The bill has since sat in the House Judiciary Committee, supposedly held in a backlog by the Watergate business and since then by the massive bill (S. 1) which would have rewritten a large portion of federal crime statutes. It is uncertain when the legislation might be adopted, but it has been endorsed by most major national leaders, including ex-President Ford.[21]

Although there are relatively few specific pressure groups that would benefit from the legislation, it may be viewed by legislators as a program which would be generally popular, and apparently would not hurt anyone. The public popularity of such a program was tested in1966, before victim compensation became an issue of which many people were aware. A poll taken on behalf of the President's Commission on Law Enforcement and Administration of Justice revealed that about 60 percent of the responses were favorable to public compensation and about 30 percent were opposed.[22] Given the increased concern about the extent of crime in the last decade, the results of a similar survey today might even be more favorable. There is general sympathy for victims of crime, and legislators perceive this emotion. The compensation program would indeed do something for some innocent victims of crime. The inefficient aspects of the program are of such a subtle nature that they probably would not be linked to the program by many individuals, so there does not appear to be any group that is likely to oppose the bill.[23]

Two groups that would appear to benefit from compensation, but are likely to have little political input, are judges and criminals. Over time, judges have seemed less willing to send criminals to prison, as evidenced by the general trend of a falling prison population in relation to the nation's population.[24] This may partly be due to the extensive use of plea bargaining, the actions of parole boards, and expanded use of probation. If crime victims receive payments, the deeds of criminals may seem less grievous and may politically justify the sentences given to criminals. Such sentences are viewed as too lenient by some, and are an important political issue.[25] Criminals would, of course, directly benefit from any general reduction in prison sentences. Another manner in which criminals would benefit, although it would make little difference in practice, is that the incentive of a victim to sue a criminal for civil damages to recover the costs of a crime would be reduced, simply because it would be cheaper and easier for a victim to collect from the state. Also, to the degree that moral scruples deter crime and the extent of damages inflicted on victims, the consciences of criminals may be eased by the knowledge that victims may be partially compensated for the damge inflicted in the commission of crimes.

Incentives of Politicians Implementing Compensation Programs

The public-choice theory of bureaucracy provides guidance for predicting how the participants in a public program can be expected to act.[26] The primary prediction that can be made about the compensation plan is that it will grow rapidly after initiation. The bill which passed the Senate in 1973 would have appropriated $5 million for the implementation of the program. That amount was based on the recommendation of the LEAA study. The appropriation was raised to $40 million in 1977 by H.R. 7010. Clearly the budget would increase rapidly in subsequent years, as the federal government would be obligated to pay for the expenses of federal administrators, claims arising in federal jurisdictions, and up to 50 percent of expenses incurred by states giving compensation that meets the guidelines set down by the federal agency.

In the last few years, many states have implemented and funded compensation programs. Some, possibly most, of these programs were implemented in anticipation of the federal subsidy that would be received when the compensation bill passed Congress. This was definitely the case in Rhode Island, Louisiana, and in Illinois, which ". . . enacted a victim compensation statute in 1973, but the legislature failed to appropriate funds to support the program, thus, presumably, keeping it in limbo, perhaps until federal funds are forthcoming."[27] The states which currently do not have compensation programs could be expected to adopt them in response to the heavy federal subsidy. Presumably they would receive assistance in establishing programs from the Department of Justice, which would directly benefit from the number of states with programs as well as from the scope of the program nationally.

The incentives for state legistlators to support victim compensation are easy to discern. If they do not support compensation they allow federal tax dollars to be shifted from their state residents to states which have the program. The federal subsidy reduces the price to a state of providing a compensation program.[28] This is illustrated in figure 4-1, which is an adaptation of Niskanen's bureaucracy model, including the modifications suggested for this model by Breton and Wintrobe.[29] Readers unfamiliar with this model can see Appendix B for a review.

The vertical axis in figure 4-1 measures the expenditures (including administrative costs) per compensation provided by a state. The horizontal axis measures the number of awards given in one fiscal year in any state. Hence, the total expenditures on compensation in one state will be the number of awards in that state times the average outlay on each award in the state. Curve DH is the marginal-valuation or demand curve of state legislators for victim compensation. The BM curve is the marginal-cost curve of the bureau providing compensation payments to the victims of crime.[30]

The producers of compensation would like to fully exploit their budget potential, which is constrained at the margin by DH. In this Niskanen-world, the number of awards would be at the point where total cost (the area under

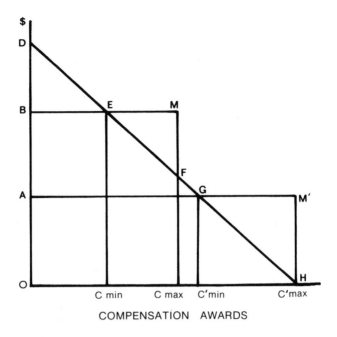

Figure 4-1. State Expenditures on Compensation

the marginal-cost curve) and total budget are equal. This would yield C_{max} number of compensations with budget $OBMC_{max}$ $(=ODFC_{max})$. Accepting the most restrictive assumptions posited by Breton and Wintrobe, so that politicians could completely control the bureaucracy at no cost, the number of compensations would be C_{min}. This would yield a budget of $OBEC_{min}$, the smallest possible budget that could emerge. The actual budget would be likely to lie somewhere between C_{min} and C_{max}.

Once the federal program is implemented, and the federal government pays 50 percent of the outlays of the state programs, the marginal cost of compensation falls to one-half of its actual level from the perspective of the state legislators, and would be perceived as curve AM'. The real expenditure remains the BM level, but the cost to state decision-makers becomes AM'. In this case the Niskanen model yields a C'_{max} level of output with budget $OAM'C'_{max}$, while the most restrictive Breton and Wintrobe assumptions yield a C'_{min} number of compensations with budget $OAGC'_{min}$.[31]

The number of awards may be H, all compensations the legislators believe are beneficial. If such were the position achieved, as seen in figure 4-2, the state legislature would allocate budget $OAM'C'_{max}$ for the purchase of H compensations. The federal government would pay $ABJM'$, 50 percent of the entire outlay, $OBJC'_{max}$ (ignoring administrative costs).

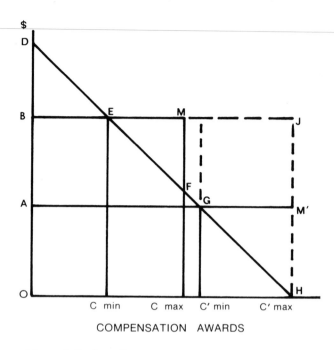

Figure 4-2. State Expenditures with Federal Subsidy

Many states have not implemented compensation programs on their own volition because the expenditures outweigh the benefits perceived by the legislators, as seen in figure 4-3, where the cost curve lies above all points on the marginal-valuation curve. With federal subsidization, the price of providing awards to victims as seen by legislators falls from B to A. Then they would have the incentive to begin such a program, which will give at least C'_{min} number of compensations. It is unlikely that any state would have a demand curve so low that even with federal subsidization the cost would still be too high to allow compensation by the state. The legislators are faced with the choice of financing compensation to get the federal subsidy or allowing their constituents to pay federal taxes for the programs in other states.[32]

A budget estimate of over $.5 billion for a nationwide compensation system was derived previously. This estimate was made under the assumption that compensation was instituted in every state and at the federal level, and that each state reached a level of awards projected by existing state programs. But the latter did not reflect the subsidy effect on the size of the program. Once the impact of the 50 percent subsidy is taken into account, the states would be found to engage in more compensation than they would have without federal assistance. As figure 4-1 shows, without assistance a state would provide between C_{min} and C_{max} compensations, but with federal assistance the number

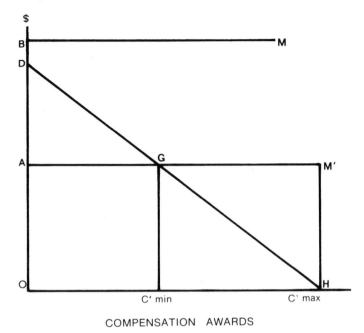

Figure 4-3. Incentives to Implement State Compensation Programs

would rise to C'_{min} at the least, and possibly as high as C'_{max}. Assuming unitary elasticity of demand (that is, if price falls by half, quantity purchased doubles) on the part of the legislators for compensation, the program would double in size in each state, which would mean a national compensation budget of over $1 billion annually.

This would be achieved by increasing the size of the average compensation payment as well as by increasing the number of compensation awards granted in each state. Without federal subsidies, some states pay an average of $4,000 per compensation (some with lower maximum payments than allowed by the federal guideline). With a 50 percent federal subsidy, if a state grants $8,000 per award, the cost to the state remains at $4,000. A state could also continue to make awards average $4,000, but make two times the number of payments, and the federal subsidy would leave the cost to the state constant. What would emerge in practice is uncertain, probably some combination of the two extremes. The important point displayed by the Niskanen model is the potential for growth of the compensation programs that could occur due to the impact of the subsidy feature.

It is worth noting here the importance of the percent size of a federal subsidy. If the federal subsidy of the state program were 75 percent rather than

50 percent, the cost to the federal government could triple, not just increase by the difference between 50 and 75 percent, which would seem to indicate only a 50 percent increase in the subsidy. The reason for the tripling of the costs to the federal government is that with a 75 percent subsidy a state only pays one-quarter of the costs. Hence, if the states were to spend $2 billion on compensation, they would receive $1.5 billion from the federal government, costing the states $.5 billion. This is compared to the 50 percent subsidy, by which if the states spend $1 billion on compensation, they would receive $.5 billion from the federal government, costing the states $.5 billion.

Incentives of Government Officials Operating Compensation Programs

Once public compensation became nationwide, those in charge of operating the programs would have incentives to expand the programs, so as to enhance the power of their bureaus and the prestige and pay of their own positions. The federal bureau operating the subsidy program would have no incentive to reduce the growth of the state bureaus, since they have concurrent incentives.[33] These motives are not inconsistent with the motives of the victims and their lawyers, who will want to receive the largest awards possible as often as possible.

Although the authors of the LEAA and CBO studies believed that the compensation program would grow very little, that assumption is difficult to accept, considering the motives of government officials and the history of other bureaus. The growth of other independent commissions which handle various types of claims may provide some evidence as to the possible growth rate of the compensation program.

The Occupational Safety and Health Review Commission was established by a December 1970 act of Congress. In fiscal 1972, the first full year of operation, the commission had twenty-three employees and a $400,000 budget.[34] By fiscal 1977, the appropriation had grown to $6.3 million for a staff of 175, which was used to review about 4,000 cases in that year. On a somewhat smaller scale, the Indian Claims Commission, which hears and adjudicates the claims of Indians, grew from twenty-two employees in 1965 to forty-four in fiscal 1977. The budget increased from $313,000 to $1.5 million in the same period. It was estimated that the commission completed review of 438 claims during fiscal 1975. For both of these commissions, the total average cost per claim examined was between $1,500 and $2,000. The National Labor Relations Board, which has had a nearly constant number of employees over the past decade, had its budget triple in that time to $82 million in fiscal 1977. This was allocated to cover about 52,000 unfair labor practices and representation cases, for an average administrative cost of $1,500 per case examined (in all aspects) during the year.

The average claim-cost figures of these commissions are not necessarily comparable to the costs that would be incurred by compensation commissions, but the general administrative expense appears to be higher for other quasi-judicial bodies than one might guess based on the LEAA and CBO reports. If the administrative expense per case were only $400, far below the expenses incurred by some existing federal bureaus, then 100,000 cases would cost $40 million to administer nationally, as estimated previously. Although this figure may not be very accurate, it does not seem unreasonably high, based on the performance of other bureaus charged with investigating and settling claims cases. Adding these administrative costs to the estimate made earlier of $400 million in compensation would yield a total expense of $440 million.

State victim compensation programs are relatively new in operation. The incentives that bureaus have to expand have been amply demonstrated by the theoretical models of bureaucracy and the empirical evidence that exists.[35] Some have been able to expand rapidly in their first few years of operation, so that they have not had to resort to arguing for an expansion of functions to justify budget increases. Many have not grown as fast as would be expected because many are simply awaiting federal assistance. If federal subsidies are forthcoming, the growth of such state bureaus would be likely to accelerate.

After the programs are well established, the desire for continued growth may induce the bureaus to fight for expansion for responsibilities. If the crime rate continues to increase as it has in the past two decades the bureaus will experience a continued natural expansion. There are three other aspects of normal operation that will enable the bureaus to take full advantage of their positions, given existing conditions. First, unlike private insurance companies, the compensation boards have little reason to prevent all but the most blatant fraud. Second, given the positions of lawyers in the operation of these programs, there will be incentives to bring more and more cases to the boards for consideration and to work for the maximum compensation. Third, the public would require a certain amount of time to become aware of the compensation program, so that information dissemination would yield increased claims.

Numerous articles by legal scholars have expressed concern that fraud would be a problem, the prevention of which would require vigilance by the compensation boards. Actually, fraud would not be a significant problem if it were made a felony and treated harshly when uncovered. However, the boards will experience better budgetary growth if they assume a passive role with respect to inflated claims. Moreover, since it is unpleasant and possibly politically dangerous to reject claims, administrators will be more likely to accept inflated claims than would be the case in private insurance. In a public bureau a one-dollar cut in compensation leads to a one-dollar cut in the budget. In a private enterprise the administrators who prevent fraud and padding are more likely to benefit from such efforts.[36]

It is possible that compensation boards may intentionally be blind to problems of fraud. As of the sixth full year of operation of compensation in

England, the executive secretary of the British board reported: "No case has yet come to the board's notice in which compensation was obtained by fraud, and the safeguards therefore appear to be effective."[37] This is similar to the experience of the several American states' programs, which claim to have experienced little problem with fraud. In Massachusetts:

No action has been taken against claimants because of the subsequent discovery that they recovered payments from the offenders or from some other source that duplicated compensation received earlier under the compensation statute. There is no machinery in the attorney general's office that could be adapted to monitoring or policing such abuse.

Fraud does not appear to have been a problem in administering the Massachusetts crime victim compensation program. There have been no referrals for criminal investigation or prosecution.[38]

The state of New York uses investigators in its compensation program to establish the validity of claims, and some fraudulent cases have been rejected on the basis of the investigation. But, as the chief investigator noted, "As long as someone is actually the innocent victim of a crime and his claim is bona fide, padding is not looked at particularly harshly, but we must naturally eliminate all padding. . . ." Similarly:

The Board appears to adopt an attitude of benevolent skepticism in such matters, based on the idea that the victims are after all the "good guys" and that they ought to be treated with kindness and compassion and not badgered about minor discrepancies in their claims.

The Board also takes pride in the fact that it has on occasion taken the initiative to develop a factual basis for a claim where the claimant was unable to do so.

In general the attitude is, as expressed by the chief investigator, "If we can make an award under the law, we make it."[39]

Although it is impossible and inefficient to ferret out all fraud and padded claims, the attitude of the compensation boards may be such as to encourage fraud and padding to some politically acceptable level. It may be comparable to welfare and food-stamp fraud, which are significant, but are generally not prevented until they become so large as to irritate voters and lead politicians to call for some action—which, on occasion, has been taken.[40]

The second feature of standard operating procedures that would help the boards to grow is the incentive presented to lawyers to bring numerous cases for compensation. One issue that has not been fully settled is whether the lawyers would receive some portion of their claimants' awards for their fees, or whether the lawyers would be granted fees separately. The 1973 version of the Victims of Crime Act stated:

The Board shall publish regulations providing that an attorney may, at the conclusion of the proceedings under this part, file with the Board an

appropriate statement for a fee in connection with services rendered in such proceedings.

. . . The Board shall award a fee to such attorney on substantially similar terms and conditions as is provided for the payment of representation under Section 3006A of title 18 of the United States Code.[41]

Section 3006A of Title 18 of the United States Code states, concerning the amount to be awarded attorneys, that the "court determined that reasonable attorneys' fee for successful plaintiff was $30 per in court hour and $20 per out-of-court hours, plus miscellaneous expenses reasonably incurred."[42] The Victims of Crime Act of 1977 does not discuss attorneys' fees, but appears to cover them.[43] It will be at the discretion of the states whether lawyers will be paid fees by the board for bringing cases which do not result in compensation. If they are to receive fees only for successful cases, lawyers would serve as a screening service for many cases and prevent some bad cases from going to the boards for consideration.

If fees are set as a percent of the award, lawyers will be less willing to help process small claims. There would be some minimum expected level at which lawyers would be willing to assist victims, but the decision in each case would depend upon the time involved in the particular case, the value of the lawyer's time, and the expected value of the award. There would be an incentive to make the claim as large as would be reasonable in the eyes of the boards, so as to maximize the fee and to serve as an incentive for potential claimants to engage the services of a lawyer.

If fees are awarded by the board on the basis of the work performed in the case, lawyers would be willing to bring any size case for compensation, given the expected chance of success. They would have an incentive to induce victims to bring forward all potential claims that appear compensable. If attorneys are to receive fees from the boards for all cases, successful or not, they would encourage all victims to become award claimants, yielding a staggering volume of claims. If states operate under different guidelines for fees, there will be an interesting comparison available in the future for examining the effects of the different fee methods.

A third factor that will help the compensation programs to expand naturally, although the boards can assist in this area, is that information about many compensation programs is not widespread. Hence, potential claimants could be ignorant of the possibilities of compensation, as they have been in states which currently have programs.

New York is overcoming this information problem by asking other agencies such as hospitals and police departments to refer victims to the compensation board. Lawyers can also be expected to serve as an information source for potential claimants. Furthermore, one would expect some lawyers to specialize in compensation proceedings once the program becomes large enough to encourage full-time devotion to that activity. Indeed, "there are indications

in Massachusetts and New Jersey that the advent of no-fault automobile insurance may induce the bar to increase its attention to victim compensation practice."[44]

As such natural inducements to expansion begin to diminish in impact on budgetary growth, the administrators of compensation programs can be expected to attempt to expand the functions of the boards in order to maintain the growth of their bureaus. If not already allowed in the enacting legislation or in all states with programs, one obvious manner to encourage a larger volume of claims is to allow attorneys' fees to be paid by the boards, independent of the size of the claim and independent of the success of the claim. This is argued as logical by many legal scholars, as one would expect, because "claimants truly need them [lawyers], and [otherwise] the public will be deprived of monitors to help keep boards responsive and fair."[45] Since many legislators and most judges are lawyers, the logic and equity of this argument may be obvious to them, so that it would not be surprising to see it emerge.

Another change, which could emerge legislatively or judicially, is the removal of the lower and upper limits on payments to victims. Federal legislation would set the limits at $100 and $50,000, as written currently. However, given the tragic nature of some victims' injuries and the staggering medical costs these entail, it is easy to see that the $50,000 limit will appear inadequate in a number of cases. Legislative or judicial sympathy may lead to a removal of the upper payment limit.[46] Removal of the $100 lower claim limit, which is standard in most states' compensation programs, has been called for by a former commissioner in Maryland and by others sympathetic to the plight of those victims whose losses are less than $100.[47] Such a move would expand the volume of claims received, which would increase the needed administrative staffs.

Since compensation programs are *ex gratia,* to the state they have the same status as a welfare payment. Individuals are not allowed to sue the state for compensation should the board reject a claim or be unable to accept it under existing guidelines. However, in most states with programs, as well as in the proposed federal program, judicial review of awards would be allowed. Such review will cause the boards to spend a certain amount of time in the courts defending their decisions, which would expand the range of required functions. Boards would have to weigh the relative merits of granting larger claims versus contesting the claims in court. More important though, is the possibility that by judicial decree the courts may expand the range of compensation payments for victims, even if the legislature will not. By judicial interpretation judges rewrite the law. This area has no reason to be exempt from such actions. It is certain that lawyers will attempt to expand the programs by this method.

An obvious and logical possibility for long-range expansion of compensation programs is in the area of non-pecuniary damages. Most rape victims incur small pecuniary damages, but may incur large pain and suffering costs. Only in Hawaii can victims currently receive compensation for such psychic losses, even

though they are a true cost of victimization. The proposed federal legislation does not include such awards and would not reimburse the states for any such awards. It is likely that some program administrators, lawyers, and victims would push for expansion of compensation payments into this area. Whether it happens by legislative action or by judicial fiat, potentially it would add huge sums of compensation awards, as these costs are common and sizable.

The expansion of victim compensation into noncriminal areas is a possibility for the future. If national medical care is instituted, much of the function of existing compensation programs could be eliminated. Administrators would have to find other victims to assist to keep their bureaus functioning. New Zealand absorbed its victim-compensation program into a universal accident-compensation system which "covers everyone in the country . . . for any kind of accident—no matter how or when it happens or who is at fault."[48] Traditional systems of civil liability were seen as capricious and inequitable, so the common-law right of action against tortfeasors was abolished.[49] Further expansion of compensation to cover all property losses is also under consideration in New Zealand, and was once proposed in a bill before the New York legislature. This would be a possible extension of powers for a state compensation, so further advocacy may be expected.

If such a program were expanded in scope of operation it would significantly reduce the scope of coverage by private insurance. Existing legislation, which appears to be little more than a slight expansion of the small compensation programs that exist in several states, probably poses little threat to areas now covered by private insurance. In the short run there may be some changes in the coverage of private insurance policies. Companies could offer lower rates on medical and income insurance by excluding losses that would be covered by public compensation. Much like the insurance policies that have arisen to cover losses not covered by Medicare, supplemental crime-loss policies could be offered. This would, of course, place many people under the public compensation program who would not qualify currently because they have private coverage for crime losses.

Conclusion

Public compensation is structured to have the taxpayers provide a balm for the suffering of innocent victims of crime. Once enacted it may reduce the chances for institution of a restitution program, by which criminals would make payments to their victims. If victims are compensated by the state, the demand for satisfaction from the criminals may be reduced, so that the basic problem, crime, will not be addressed.

Like many governmental programs, victim compensation is designed with the best of intentions, and has been claimed to cost relatively little to achieve

a desirable goal. In reality, victim compensation threatens to emerge as another tentacle of leviathan, encompassing far more in territory and dollars than ever envisioned. Numerous similar stories have unfolded in recent years, and victim compensation would seem unlikely to offer one additional instance of such bureaucratic growth.

Notes

1. Duane G. Harris, "Compensating Victims of Crime: Blunting the Blow," *Business Review* (Federal Reserve Board, Philadelphia, June 1972), p. 19.

2. Harris' estimate of 700,000 victims was based on figures from the FBI's *Uniform Crime Reports,* which are replaced here by the superior LEAA data. There were approximately 1.7 million victims of violent crimes in 1975, as seen in table 4-1. They would receive average payments of about $2,100 each, assuming that the cost of victimization increased at the same rate as the general price index since 1970. Price index from *Annual U.S. Economic Data,* Federal Reserve Bank of St. Louis, May 17, 1977, p. 17.

3. U.S., *Victims of Crime,* 92nd Cong., 1971 and 1972, citing: U.S., Department of Justice, Law Enforcement Assistance Administration, "Victims of Crime Act of 1972," Staff Study, Program and Management Evaluation Division (Washington, D.C.: U.S.G.P.O., 1972), pp. 719-47.

4. U.S., House, Committee on the Judiciary, *Victims of Crime Act of 1977* (Report to accompany H.R. 7010), 95th Cong., 1st sess., report no. 95-337, p. 12.

5. The figure in Maryland was expected to rise from 4.5 percent in 1974 to 7.1 percent in 1976. The 5.8 percent estimate for 1975 will be used for this estimate. Figures provided by the administrator of the Crime Victims Act of the State of Washington, correspondence of October 1974.

6. U.S., National Criminal Justice Information and Statistics Service, *Criminal Victimization in the United States: A Comparison of 1974 and 1975 Findings,* A National Crime Panel Survey Report, no. SD-NCP-N-5 (Washington, D.C.: U.S.G.P.O., February 1977), p. 56.

7. This estimate assumed that every state adopted victim compensation along the lines of the federal program. It does not assume aggressive expansion of the program, nor does it assume that more than 5.8 percent of the victims of violent crime would be compensated. This figure probably would increase over time.

8. U.S., House, Committee on the Judiciary, *Crime Victim Compensation,* Hearings, 94th Cong., 1975 and 1976, serial no. 39, p. 1273.

9. Ibid., p. 281.

10. Ibid., pp. 196-208.

11. National Criminal Justice Information and Statistics Service, *Criminal Victimization in the United States,* p. 9.

12. U.S., House, *Crime Victim Compensation,* pp. 89–108.

13. Ibid., p. 56.

14. This estimate is based on past information gathered on lawyers' income and expenses. U.S., Bureau of the Census, Census of Selected Service Industries, *1972 Subject Series–Legal Services,* SC72-5-4, (Washington, D.C.: U.S.G.P.O., 1975).

15. U.S., Senate, Committee on the Judiciary, *Victims of Crime,* Hearings, 92d Cong., 1971 and 1972, pp. 491–92.

16. According to a 1970 survey of Louis Harris and Associates, 33 percent of the individuals interviewed in a nationwide survey rated the job done by local law-enforcement officials unfavorably. U.S., National Criminal Justice Information and Statistics Service, *Sourcebook of Criminal Justice Statistics–1973,* Michael J. Hineland et al., eds. (Washington, D.C.: U.S.G.P.O., 1974), p. 134.

17. Surveys taken in thirteen large American cities on victimization in 1972 showed that between 40 and 51 percent of all crimes of violence were reported to the police. For all personal crimes the figures were even lower, ranging from 31 to 41 percent. U.S., National Criminal Justice Information and Statistics Service, *Crime in the Nation's Five Largest Cities,* A National Crime Panel Survey Report (Washington, D.C., U.S.G.P.O., 1974), p. 28; U.S., National Criminal Justice Information and Statistics Service, *Crime in Eight American Cities,* A National Crime Panel Survey Report, (Washington, D.C.: U.S.G.P.O., 1974), p. 38.

18. In 1971 there were 5.4 million offenses known by the police in 4,500 cities with a population of 105 million. Only 20.9 percent of the known offenses were cleared by the police (by arrest), and 46.5 percent of the known violent crimes were cleared by the police. Since the LEAA studies indicate that less than one-half of all crimes are reported to the police, it is likely that only about 10 percent of all offenses are cleared by arrest and that only about 20 percent of all violent crimes are cleared by arrest. National Criminal Justice Information and Statistics Service, *Sourcebook of Criminal Justice Statistics,* p. 290.

19. U.S., House, *Crime Victim Compensation,* pp. 212–16.

20. For example, see the large number of witnesses from existing state programs lobbying for the federal subsidy: U.S., House, *Victims of Crime Compensation.*

21. *Miami Herald,* June 20, 1975, p. 1 (President Ford endorses victim compensation); *H.R. 7010,* 95th Cong., 1st sess. (1977) (lists members of Judiciary Committee sponsoring victim compensation).

22. National Criminal Justice Information and Statistics Service, *Sourcebook of Criminal Justice Statistics,* p. 156.

23. The only organized opposition to the proposal that may be expected would be from private insurance companies. These companies have made no public sign of awareness or concern. Correspondence of author with six major insurance companies and numerous professional insurance organizations and

lobbying arms has revealed no interest in the issue. It is possible that interest would emerge if the program were to become nationwide. However, as currently proposed the legislation may not appear to be a threat to insurance interests.

24. The rate of court commitments as a rate per 100,000 civilian population fell in half between 1954 and 1970. Actual prison population, state and federal, fell from 212,953 in 1960 to 196,429 in 1970. The number of prisoners received from courts fell from 88,575 in 1960 to 79,351 in 1970. National Criminal Justice Information and Statistics Service, *Sourcebook of Criminal Justice Statistics,* pp. 346–47.

25. For one explanation of the phenomenon of the lack of will to punish, see James M. Buchanan, "The Samaritan's Dilemma," in *Altruism, Morality, and Economic Theory,* Edmund S. Phelps, ed. (New York: Russell Sage Foundation, 1975).

26. Gordon Tullock, *The Politics of Bureaucracy* (Washington, D.C.: Public Affairs Press, 1965); Anthony Downs, *Inside Bureaucracy* (Boston: Little, Brown & Co., 1967); and William Niskanen, *Bureaucracy and Representative Government* (Chicago: Aldine, 1971).

27. Herbert Edelhertz and Gilbert Geis, *Public Compensation to Victims of Crime* (New York: Praeger Publishers, Inc., 1974), p. 174.

28. Richard E. Wagner, *The Public Economy* (Chicago: Markham Publishing Co., 1973), pp. 66–67; Wallace E. Oates, *Fiscal Federalism* (New York: Harcourt, Brace, Jovanovich, Inc., 1972), pp. 75–78.

29. Niskanen, *Bureaucracy and Representative Government,* especially chapter 3; Albert Breton and Ronald Wintrobe, "The Equilibrium Size of a Budget-maximizing Bureau," *Journal of Political Economy* 83 (February 1975), pp. 195–207.

30. It is not obvious what the slope of the marginal-cost curve would be. It is possible that victims suffering the largest pecuniary losses could be the first to be compensated, as they would have the most incentive to seek compensation, so that subsequent awards would be smaller. This would tend to reduce the slope of the curve. Evidence from existing compensation programs does not reveal any clear pattern. For simplicity, the marginal-cost curve is considered to be horizontal in the range of operations considered here. The basic result would not be altered by assuming an upward-sloping marginal-cost curve. The marginal-cost curve also represents the average cost of the awards given in a budget period. Actual awards vary considerably, but the average award is appropriate for this analysis.

31. In terms of an income-compensated demand curve, the net effect will be to leave the average citizen no better off than before. Two distinct impacts can be recognized here. One is the substitution effect due to the subsidy from the federal government. The price of compensation provided by the state legislature declines in proportion to the subsidy, so a greater quantity of compensation will be provided to the citizens of the state. However, the income

effect will mitigate the impact of the substitution effect. Citizens' tax burdens will be increased to finance the federal subsidy.

32. Wagner, *The Public Economy,* pp. 66-67.

33. Ibid., p. 132.

34. All figures from *The Budget of the U.S. Government,* various fiscal years (Washington, D.C.: U.S.G.P.O.).

35. For example, see Thomas Borcherding, ed., *Budgets and Bureaucrats: The Origins of Government Growth,* (Durham: Duke University Press, 1977).

36. See Armen Alchian and Harold Demsetz, "Production, Information Costs, and Economic Organization," *American Economic Review* 62 (December 1972); and Ludwig von Mises, *Bureaucracy* (New Rochelle, N.Y.: Arlington House, 1969).

37. David H. Harrison, "Criminal Injuries Compensation in Britain," *American Bar Association Journal* 57 (May 1971), p. 479.

38. Edelhertz and Geis, *Public Compensation,* p. 127.

39. Ibid., pp. 49-51.

40. One of the most noted instances was the welfare-reform program in California led by Governor Reagan, which removed 176,000 recipients from the relief rolls and saved an estimated $300 million annually. *New York Times,* February 2, 1972, p. 34; August 12, 1972, p. 24. More recently there has been considerable discussion about reducing fraud in food-stamp procurement: see Kenneth W. Clarkson, *Food Stamps and Nutrition* (Washington, D.C.: American Enterprise Institute, 1975), pp. 31-32.

41. U.S. Congress, Senate, *Victims of Crime Act of 1973,* 93rd Cong., 1st sess., S. 300, p. 19.

42. *United States Code Annotated,* title 18, § 3006A, pamphlet no. 2, part 1 (St. Paul, Minn.: West Publishing Co., 1975), p. 586.

43. *H.R. 7010,* 95th Cong., 1st sess. (1977), § 4.

44. Edelhertz and Geis, *Public Compensation,* p. 278. The gradual expansion of advertising by lawyers would hasten this process.

45. Ibid.

46. The current medical-malpractice problem may encourage upper limits on payments. States are unlikely to allow multimillion-dollar awards, but may be willing to allow the costs incurred to be compensated. A type of medical no-fault insurance similar in coverage to victim compensation has been proposed by Senators Kennedy and Inouye. See "The Doctors' New Dilemma," *Newsweek,* February 10, 1975, p. 41.

47. Edelhertz and Geis, *Public Compensation,* p. 278.

48. "To Accident Victims, New Zealand Offers the Balm of Money," *Wall Street Journal,* September 16, 1975, p. 1.

49. J.L. Fahy, "The Administration of the Accident Compensation Act of 1972," *Economic Bulletin,* Canterbury Chamber of Commerce, no. 592 (Christchurch, N.Z., 1975).

5

Equity Issues in Compensation

For practical purposes it can be assumed that victims bear the costs of victimization. Given the small percentage of criminals captured for crimes committed, and the even smaller percentage that are convicted for crimes and would be capable of making restitution to their victims, it is currently believed to be unrealistic to try to impose a large portion of the costs of crime upon criminals. Because of this, many proponents of public compensation, such as ex-Justice Arthur Goldberg, believe that

It is only right that society, through a program of public compensation, recognize its obligations toward these victims. As a practical matter also, society alone is able to assist the victims of crime.[1]

Public responsibility for private costs incurred in criminal assaults is a collective community need according to supporters such as ex-Senator Mike Mansfield, who considers compensation a basic social program. "Social security, medicare, aid to dependent children, assistance for the handicapped, the aged and the blind, ideas of no-fault insurance, and national health insurance all reflect a recognition of collective societal responsibility."[2] In the political setting such equity arguments are valid, and, as will be seen, must constitute the primary defense for public compensation as now proposed.

Rather than assume that Goldberg, Mansfield, and scores of politicians and writers are objective, sympathetic observers who have settled the equity justification for public compensation, this chapter develops more scientific, albeit normative, equity arguments. It considers public compensation at the constitutional and postconstitutional stages. The times of potential acceptance will be considered within the framework both of Rawls's contract theory and Bentham's utilitarianism.

Efficiency vs. Equity?

While one does not have to believe that public compensation, as currently proposed, is inefficient, it is necessary that one accept a simple trade-off that helps to generate such a conclusion. When insurance premiums (taxes paid to support public compensation), whether regressive, proportional, or progressive in structure, are based on income levels, rather than on revealed preferences for

65

risk averseness to criminal attack, individuals will consider insurance free at the margin. The next chapter develops why people will trade less self-protection for more public compensation for losses suffered in criminal attacks.

There is, of course, a limit to this effect. Individuals are assumed not to like the physical and psychic suffering incurred in criminal attacks, which are generally not compensated, or are only partially compensated by an insurance scheme. However, public insurance will lead risk-averse individuals to consume somewhat less self-protection, due to the coverage for pecuniary losses incurred in crimes. As long as this simple trade-off is accepted and understood, the general inefficiency of the compensation program is not necessarily important when considering equity issues. Equity considerations can override efficiency considerations, and may do so for certain forms of victim compensation.

Constitutional Consideration

Assume that a society is at the constitution-making stage, which is a contractual process where "the alternatives for choice are institutional arrangements that are presumed to remain in being over a succession of time period."[3] At the constitutional stage individuals are assumed to be ignorant of their future income, wealth, and *personality position* in the society for which they are considering institutional structures. By *personality position* is meant that each person is uncertain as to his future physical and psychological makeup, such factors as size, sex, color, intelligence, and preferences.[4] This is decision-making in a Rawlsian veil of ignorance, which is akin to the situation posited by Buchanan and Tullock in *The Calculus of Consent,* where "the individual, at the time of constitutional choice, is uncertain as to his own role on particular issues in the future."[5]

It seems quite plausible that the individual members of a society would believe that criminal attacks would be unjust. Crime therefore would be considered a social and economic institution that creates varying degrees of injustice. The extent of injustice (victimization) suffered by any particular individual would vary with such factors as background (parentage), current economic status, and individual fear of or risk aversion to crime. Within such a setting, it seems reasonable to assume that all individuals would favor some controls on crime. That issues of criminal justice would be considered at the constitutional level is noted by Rawls, who said that "the interest in the integrity of the person is another [fundamental interest] . . . freedom from . . . physical assault" is a concern there.[6]

When considering the decision process at the constitutional stage, and later at the postconstitutional stage, it is important not to fall into the traditional trap of the benevolent dictator. Some scholars contend that Rawls's contract theory can be improved upon by the use of a perfectly sympathetic

observer to help society achieve *Social Excellence.*[7] In the guise of Rawlsian fairness as justice, the sympathetic observer is nothing more than a return to the device of the benevolent dictator, which is inconsistent with the fundamental concepts of a democratic society. Sympathetic observers creating social-welfare functions to determine the distribution of income are to be "all who are in this difficult business of social evaluation."[8] On the other hand, Rawls incorporates Wicksell's unanimity criterion for postconstitutional choices.[9] This displays the complete divergence of his contract theory from the device of the benevolent dictator, even if it is cloaked in the form of the sympathetic observer.

While it is easy to slip into the role of the sympathetic observer, one can avoid that by using a framework consistent with fundamental concepts of fairness. This analysis presumably will be close to that used by a person in the veil of ignorance, as he thinks about the society in which he will function. While normative in nature, as is any criterion for judgment, to date this foundation is the most consistent with democratic ideals that has been developed.[10]

At the constitutional level it is likely that general rules regarding criminal actions would be formed. A specific public-compensation program for crime victims would not be formulated, but the basic responsibility of all participants—the state, potential criminals, and potential victims—would be outlined. Rawls believes that men would agree that man in a democratic society should be free to protect himself and to lead a personal life-style as he wishes. The role of self-respect enters here, as man is assumed to have integrity for himself and for others.

It could be advocated that fairness implies that the rights assigned to the individual shall not be violated by others, without redress to the offended individual. When one involuntarily surrenders some of his rights to another, the rights thief must be willing to accept whatever consequences have been stipulated by society. The offended individual, the victim, incurs costs in the involuntary loss of rights, for which he should be compensated by the offender, who has taken these rights without prior agreement. It seems that the offender, not the members of society, should make restitution to the offended.

Under the rules of our legal system, if a visitor were to fall down the steps of the host's house due to worn carpeting, the visitor would be more likely to receive restitution from the host than if an assailant had pushed him down a flight of steps and then stolen his wallet. The former case falls in the category of tort law. The latter case is unlikely to go beyond criminal law. The victim would be more likely to receive restitution in the accidental case. The price paid for the malicious act may be less than that paid for personal negligence. With the malicious act, although the cost borne by the victim may be greater than the cost incurred due to negligence, restitution by the criminal would be to society as a whole, probably as a period of probation and/or a small fine.[11]

From the view of society, there is a clear difference between the above two cases. In the negligence case, there was no specific attempt to injure anyone,

while in the malicious incident there was. Society wishes to discourage such behavior by criminal-justice procedures. The fairness of paying the victim for the costs he suffered due to negligence also seems clear. However, is it fair that the victim is less likely to recover for the costs he suffered when pushed down the stairs? It is likely that most would agree that this violates basic concepts of fairness.

Who should bear the costs incurred in criminal attacks? Fairness would dictate that the criminal bear the burden of his actions. If the criminal is unknown (as is true in most cases), then who should bear the burden, the victim or his fellow citizens? This is the critical question, which probably would not be resolved at the constitutional stage, as that process is likely to consider general liability for criminal acts. However, the constitutional process may make provisions for assistance for victims of criminal acts as part of an overall plan to assist some unfortunate members of society.

Individual freedom includes the ability to expose oneself to various levels of danger at different times and places. One should be free to walk the streets of the Bronx at night if one wishes, but who should bear the probable costs of such an act? In a society with some individual freedom, a certain amount of crime will exist, and is likely to exist in varying levels at different places. Hence, the individual right of self-protection is important. All individuals engage in some self-protection, but all have different attitudes toward the possibility of victimization.

In the veil of ignorance, the potential citizen recognizes that different attitudes will exist in the society in which he will participate. While he would not impose severe restrictions on private actions, he may not wish to subsidize the actions of others or expect his own actions to be subsidized. However, realizing that some crime is nearly random in nature with respect to the victim, and that the victim could not reasonably have been expected to have prevented his misfortune, some assistance may be deemed desirable, as all citizens have some chance of incurring such misfortune. Random victimization is similar to natural disasters that no one could have been reasonably expected to foresee or prevent. Rawlsian justice may lead to assistance for such occurrences. All potential citizens would foresee identical probabilities of being struck by random misfortune, and may prefer to make provisions for such instances.

Most random disasters result in relatively small costs which can be borne by the victim. Individuals can either bear the full costs of the misfortune at the time of occurrence or spread the costs over time by purchasing insurance. However, few individuals can afford very costly tragedies, or could be expected to carry insurance sufficient to cover the costs of such incidents. Hence, it is possible that potential citizens would opt for assistance to victims of severe tragedies, because it can be assumed that no one would voluntarily subject himself to such a position.[12]

It is unlikely that state aid for victims of smaller tragedies would be adopted. Although some victimization at this level is also random, preferences

play a more important role. It is predictable that some individuals will expose themselves to higher levels of low-cost danger than will others. These victims would be expected to care for themselves, rely on private charity, or would be implicitly aided by the adoption of the difference principle of income distribution.[13] This principle, which Rawls believes would be agreed upon as just at the constitutional level, allows for the most unfortunate to be able to afford some self-protection and insurance. The difference principle of income distribution would insure that no one would be incapable of securing some self-assistance to cover losses to criminal assault and other unfortunate incidents.[14]

This income assurance would not mean that all individuals would purchase complete self-protection, but it would insure that all would be capable of normal self-protection. How individuals behaved beyond this basic ability to be secure would be at the discretion of each person. Some individuals in all income classes will be relatively less risk averse than the general populace, so that, in the eyes of their fellow citizens, they will be foolish with their own safety.

At the constitutional stage the citizen would realize that in the future he may be a foolish individual who will expose himself to "too much" danger. Rather than encourage such behavior by offering payments to cover the costs incurred by himself and others, one is likely to prefer that the foolish individual, even if that be himself, bear the costs of his actions. Knowing that there is a chance that he may be foolish, he may wish to constrain such behavior in advance.

Just as the citizen may believe that he would be better off in the long run if he is forced to contribute to a fund for his old age, rather than be allowed the ability to spend all his income prior to retirement, he may support constraints on individual behavior with respect to potential danger from crime. This could be partially accomplished by requiring individuals to purchase insurance that would cover some of the costs incurred in criminal attacks. This would prevent him from being able to pass on the costs of his foolish actions to charitable individuals or to the state. This would also make foolish actions more costly because, to a certain extent, private-insurance premiums are tied to preferences for risk aversion. The foolish individual would eventually pay a penalty in high premiums for his actions, which would provide an incentive for him to limit such behavior. Beyond that, if an individual is so foolish as to wish to purposely expose himself to grave danger, then probably little would be done, except that the state may provide compensation if high costs were incurred.

Postconstitutional Consideration

Whatever evolves in the postconstitutional state is reality and must be accepted. Wishing for what might have been is of little value. In the postconstitutional consideration of public payments to the victims of crime, it should be noted that as the justice system now exists, most of the costs of victimization are

borne by the victims. The constitutional process placed the liability on the criminal, but as the system evolved the burden has fallen largely on the victims. For policy analysis, equity issues require consideration of particular proposals within a defined institutional framework that happens to exist at that time. In this framework are various redistribution models based on utility interdependence or rational selfishness.

There are pure self-interest motives which would lead some individuals to believe that a public-compensation program would be just. First there is the insurance motive. This motive is applied partially in a veil of ignorance, in that one may think, "What if I become more susceptible to crime in the future?" Individuals may support compensation now even though it will not benefit them presently but may in the future. This motive probably would not be strong for victim compensation as private insurance is available. If one assumes that public compensation would be more costly than private provision of the same service, then private insurance would be preferred.[15]

Secondly, there is a self-protection motive. This has been applied to welfare payments and other transfer programs, which some contend may exist in order to "buy off" those who otherwise may rebel due to their positions in the income distribution. Given the relative smallness of public compensation, it is difficult to imagine this rationale playing a role here. However, criminals would probably support public compensation for this reason. If citizens are compensated when victimized they are likely to make less effort to prevent crimes from occurring.

Third, there is a producer self-interest motive. That is, those who will directly benefit from the adoption of the program because they will be involved in producing the service will advocate the program. This will not cause a large number of individuals to favor any one program, but in the case of victim compensation the benefits perceived have led lawyers, bureaucrats, and other interest groups to support the program, as discussed previously.

The final motive in this category is that the public program may be a substitute for private programs. If one is covered by public insurance then there is less reason to purchase private insurance, especially insurance that would cover the same costs. This rationale is likely to generate support only from those who believe they will receive a net transfer from the program, which would probably be a minority of the citizens in this case. As long as the median voter does not perceive net transfers from the program it will be defeated.

Such motives of narrow self-interest cannot be considered equity arguments, with the possible exception of the insurance motive. While they may explain the support for victim compensation from some group of individuals, they do not constitute fairness arguments, as can the utility-interdependence explanations of equity.

The primary grounds for consideration of postconstitutional transfers within existing institutions are provided by Pareto-optimal redistribution models based on utility interdependence.[16] In such models it is assumed that some indi-

viduals receive positive utility from transferring portions of their income or wealth to another individual or group of individuals, who may or may not be specified. Here the concern is with the specific utility interdependence of compensation to crime victims, where the increment to the utility of the benefactors depends upon the consumption of that specific service.

Most individuals probably do have sympathy for the victims of criminal assaults. Two polls in the mid-1960s indicated about 60 percent of the respondents favored state assistance for the victims of serious criminal acts.[17] An even greater number might have sympathized with the situation faced by the victims, but happened to oppose state assistance.

Individuals may decide that reducing the burden of victimization by reducing the crime rate may not be worth the investment, so that they would be willing to aid members of society who become innocent victims of crime. Traditionally it was believed that a compensation program would be almost strictly for low-income individuals. The LEAA Staff Report in 1972 claimed that "97 percent of violent crimes are inflicted on people whose income is less than $10,000 per year." The 1970 census displayed 49.1 percent of the population to have family incomes over $10,000.[18] The belief in greater rates of victimization of low-income individuals is not supported by the findings of the victimization surveys taken by the LEAA. They reported that for all crimes against persons, whites and blacks, the victimization rate was higher for individuals with family incomes over $10,000.[19]

Since higher-income individuals do have more health and income insurance, the incidence of their usage of state compensation might well be lower than that of low-income individuals, especially if a needs test is applied to claimants. However, if insurance purchasers were to buy policies excluding the costs incurred in criminal attacks, the usage by higher-income individuals would rise. Hence, it is not possible to tell if a public compensation program would constitute a subsidy for low-income individuals, as claimed by most proponents. With compensation, the burden of crime with respect to the income position of the victims may not change significantly.

If it is true that there is a collective desire to provide assistance for the victims of crime, the group providing the subsidy might desire to give the aid in a manner different from the program now proposed. If the primary purpose of the program is to insure that all citizens are covered for some of the losses incurred due to crime, the most efficient transfer may be a direct-dollar transfer based on some form of negative-income-tax scale, with a mandatory insurance requirement.[20] The income recipients may prefer to receive a cash transfer and not purchase insurance, or at least spend only a fraction of the transfer on insurance. However, the utility interdependence is based on the recipients' consumption of a specific service, insurance.

Most discussion of equity has been in terms of vertical equity. Horizontal equity has been discussed much less, but seems to be of importance in this issue. Two individuals of the same income level are not equal if one has suffered a

major crime attack during the year. Because they are not the same they should not be treated the same. In the context of horizontal equity, the rich man who has been injured by a crime has the same right to compensation as does the poor man. This consideration raises questions about the equity of needs tests for victims of crime. If the victim compensation is to be insurance, then the rich man, who has paid his share of taxes to support the program, should benefit like the poor man when he suffers losses in criminal attacks.

If a public-compensation program were believed preferable to a subsidized private plan, then equity and efficiency would require alterations in the proposed program. A program with a $100 deductible and free legal assistance insures that individuals who are relatively less risk averse, and therefore incur the most amount of crime, will benefit disproportionately from the program. For the same tax payment as a person of equal income, the person who is less risk averse will receive greater benefits.[21] There is no way to prevent this from occurring in such a program as this one. To a certain extent the efficiency considerations are to be overridden by the fairness issue. However, it is possible to construct a program so that excessive usage of the benefits would be discouraged.

First, the deduction could be made larger, so that a victim who suffers large numbers of attacks would incur heavy costs per attack, which would give him an incentive to be more risk averse to crime. Second, co-insurance could be adopted so that victims pay a percentage of the total cost beyond the deduction. If the pecuniary loss were estimated to be $1,000 beyond the deductible, then the state may pay 90 percent or some other portion of the costs, so that victims would have incentives to hold down the size of possible losses. Third, payments could decline in size due to an increasing deductible and smaller state co-insurance percentages with each claim filed within a certain time period. Given these provisions, victim-prone individuals would find victimization incidents more and more costly, but individuals who are more risk averse would be likely to receive a fuller portion of the costs. Fourth, the upper limit on payments could be removed. The victims who suffer the most damaging attacks will only be helped to a limited extent by a program with a maximum payment of, say, $50,000. Few individuals can afford to carry insurance sufficient to cover the costs incurred should they become incapacitated for life. Since no one would intentionally place himself in such a position, they may be the most deserving of assistance.

While these policy suggestions are normative and are based on efficiency grounds, they are also consistent with what may be considered traditional norms of fairness. The effect of the program would be to assist deserving victims, but would not encourage behavior which leads to more victimization.

Notes

1. Arthur Goldberg, "Preface" (Symposium on Victim Compensation), *Southern California Law Review* 43 (1970), p. 2.

2. Mike Mansfield, "Justice for the Victims of Crime," *Houston Law Review* 9 (September 1971), p. 79.

3. James M. Buchanan and Winston Bush, "Political Constraints on Contractual Redistribution," *American Economic Review* 64 (May 1974), p. 153.

4. John Rawls, *A Theory of Justice* (Cambridge: Harvard University Press, 1971), pp. 136-42.

5. James M. Buchanan and Gordon Tullock, *The Calculus of Consent* (Ann Arbor: Ann Arbor Press, 1962), p. 191.

6. John Rawls, "Reply to Alexander and Musgrave," *Quarterly Journal of Economics* 88 (November 1974), p. 640.

7. Sidney S. Alexander, "Social Evaluation through National Choice," *Quarterly Journal of Economics* 88 (November 1974), pp. 597-624.

8. Ibid., p. 619.

9. Rawls, *A Theory of Justice*, pp. 282-84.

10. The best and most comprehensive source in this area is the award-winning book by James M. Buchanan, *The Limits of Liberty: Between Anarchy and Leviathan* (Chicago: University of Chicago Press, 1975).

11. It should be noted that in the malicious incident the victim probably would have the right to sue for damages in tort, but the incident of this is so rare as to be unimportant in the operation of the criminal-justice system. Linden discusses this point in "Victims of Crime and Tort Law," and considers some empirical evidence. One reason for this difference is that homeowners or some other form of liability insurance would assist the party being sued for negligence, so that a suit would be more worthwhile than in the case of the criminal act, which insurance will not cover.

12. It is also possible that potential citizens would favor no state assistance for victims of severe tragedies, believing themselves to be generous enough to provide for the needs of the unfortunate by private charity. However, individuals may not wish to chance the charitable instincts of their fellow citizens. See Gordon Tullock, "The Charity of the Uncharitable," *Western Economic Journal* 9 (December 1971), pp. 379-92.

13. See Rawls, *A Theory of Justice,* pp. 75-83 for a discussion of this principle and pp. 152-57 for an explanation of the maximin principle, which Rawls believes would emerge.

14. For an exposition of this concept in more general terms, see James M. Buchanan, "A Hobbesian Interpretation of the Rawlsian Difference Principle," *Kyklos* 29 (1976), pp. 5-25.

15. The empirical evidence that exists tends to confirm the hypothesis that publicly provided goods cost more than private alternatives. See *Budgets and Bureaucrats: The Origins of Government Growth,* Thomas Borcherding, ed. (Durham: Duke University Press, 1977).

16. See Harold Hockman and James D. Rodgers, "Pareto Optimal Redistribution," *American Economic Review* 59 (September 1969), pp. 542-57.

17. U.S., National Criminal Justice Information and Statistics Service, *Sourcebook of Criminal Justice Statistics—1973.* Ed. by Michael Hindeland

et al. (Washington, D.C.: U.S.G.P.O., 1974), pp. 347–48; Herbert Edelhertz and Gilbert Geis, *Public Compensation to Victims of Crime* (New York: Praeger Publishers, Inc., 1974), p. 289.

18. U.S., Senate, Committee on the Judiciary, *Victims of Crime—1972,* citing Staff Study, "Victims of Crime Act of 1972," p. 737.

19. The 1974 and 1975 victimization surveys report that individuals with family incomes under $10,000 suffered more crimes of violence, per capita, than did individuals with family incomes over $10,000, but that higher-income individuals suffered more crimes of theft, so that the highest aggregate-victimization rate was suffered by individuals with family incomes over $25,000. Individuals in the under-$10,000 income category comprised 43.3 percent of the population in 1975 and suffered 48.5 percent of the crimes of violence. U.S., National Criminal Justice Information and Statistics Service, *Criminal Victimization in the United States: A Comparison of 1974 and 1975 Findings,* report no. SD-NCP-N-5 (Washington, D.C.: U.S.G.P.O., 1977), p. 18.

20. The welfare-reform program proposed by President Carter in 1977 would be a step in this direction, in that it would be more oriented to direct-cash grants in lieu of in-kind transfers to the poor. It does not, however, deal with insurance. *New York Times,* August 7, 1977, p. 1.

21. To a certain extent the same criticism can be made of private insurance.

6

Moral Hazard and
Victim Compensation

To this point the study of public compensation for crime victims has not included a formal economic analysis, in the sense of a traditional microeconomic examination of the major variables. This chapter considers victim compensation from the perspective with which an economist would be likely to view a public-policy problem. This chapter is intended to help construct a method of considering public insurance, a topic which has not been extensively developed.

The model developed here examines, from a utility-maximizing framework, the process by which individuals rationally trade hazard for other goods. The limits to hazard and the rate at which it will be traded for other goods are determined by legal institutions, customs, and individual preferences. Assuming such environmental variables as given, this analysis considers how individuals react to changes in institutional frameworks concerning the costs of victimization.

The moral-hazard problem plays an important role here. Moral hazard is the effect of insurance on incentives. While it would be desirable for insurance to have no effect on the probability of an insured event, in general that is not possible.[1] For instance, the probability that one's house will be burglarized depends in part upon the extent of one's insurance against losses to burglary. The term moral hazard can be misleading. The word moral has a normative connotation about the actions that are in question. That is of no interest to the problem being considered here; the interest is in the hazard as it manifests itself toward economic phenomena, but not in the ethical evaluation of individual behavior in situations involving risk.[2]

The model initially considers a utility-maximizing individual who can purchase private insurance to cover some of the costs of victimization and can buy private goods and services which will help prevent criminal attacks upon himself. Public insurance will then be introduced, so that the two basic positions of a representative individual can be considered, first, in a regime of private insurance, and second, in a regime of public and private insurance. The model is then extended to a multiperson world to display the impact of insurance as a public good. Public insurance for the victims of crime is considered under two sets of extreme assumptions for the representative individuals: equal preferences and different incomes, and different preferences and equal incomes. This allows for an analysis of collective insurance under the full range of possible circumstances. This presentation provides a study of the logical reactions of utility-maximizing individuals to a program of publicly provided victim compensation under standard assumptions about individual behavior.

75

Basic Model

Assume a world of individuals faced with the same institutional constraints: the existence of crime, the availability of private crime insurance, and the ability to purchase private goods and services which will reduce the likelihood of crime. The utility-maximizing individual considered here has neither special nor uniform tastes; he has "normal" or "rational" tastes. All goods considered here are normal goods to the individual, in his current budget range. That is, this individual does not like to suffer the costs of crime. If the prices allow, he will purchase insurance to spread out the monetary burdens of victimization and will engage in activities which will reduce the probability of criminal assault.

For simplicity, assume that the individual has a set income or endowment, B, which is his budget per time period. All income is spent in the current time period. The goods that can be purchased by the individual are C, an all-purpose consumption good, and A, all private goods and services designed to reduce the probability of crime and private insurance for losses to crime. The other expense which enters the individual's budget is his expected loss from crime per period not covered by private insurance.

An individual faces an array of possible crimes, each of which has an array of possible costs. For simplicity, assume the individual has enough information about crimes and their costs that he estimates a net probability for the occurrence of all crimes, p, and a net average loss per L. Then in any one time period the individual would expect to lose pL to crime in monetary expenses. That is, if he expects a \$1,000 loss with a 0.1 probability, he expects to lose an average of \$100 per time period to criminal attacks. This loss can be altered in manner of time distribution by purchasing private insurance. Depending on the amount of private insurance purchased, the individual will receive a payment of some value, V, should he be the victim of a criminal attack. When the individual purchases insurance the monetary value of his expected loss to crime is reduced by the value of the expected payment from the insurance company, so that net expected loss to crime would be $p(V-L)$. This sum must always be negative, so that expected losses to crime are positive. No one can expect to make money by being a victim. This assumption is realistic because insurance policies almost always have deductibles and/or co-insurance features, so that the loss to crime, L, will always exceed the value of the insurance payment, V.

Figure 6-1 displays the utility-maximizing position of the individual with respect to the trade-off that exists between the all-purpose consumption good and preventive activity, given his budget.

Introducing Public Insurance. Having established the individual's equilibrium that would exist in the simplified world constructed here, a complication can be added to display the impact of public crime insurance on the individual.

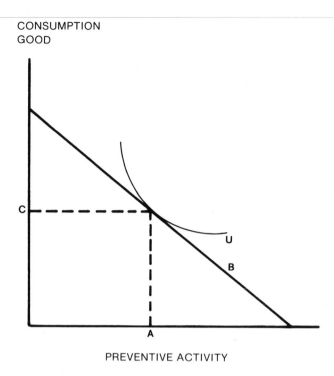

Figure 6-1. Utility Maximizing Position of the Individual

This will be a simplified version of the victim-compensation program examined in this study, but it will not differ in its basic effect.

Assume that at the beginning of a time period, in which an individual is about to decide upon the composition of his budget, that a public-insurance program is instituted. Public insurance would cover some of the same area covered by existing private insurance, for individuals who happened to own such insurance. For the public insurance, just as for private insurance, the individual will have an expected insurance payment per crime suffered, R. For simplicity it is assumed that the individual faces a constant-rate proportional income tax imposed to pay for the public-insurance program. Given the tax rate, t, the individual faces a tax bill of tB.

The particulars of the tax structure used here are unimportant because the tax bill is assumed to be insignificant in its income effect on all the variables in the individual's budget, and because the tax bill the individual pays for the public insurance he receives is unrelated to any other action he takes. There are no substitution effects between tB and any variable. All decisions made regarding quantities of various commodities to consume will not be affected by

tB. This assumption, that price for public insurance is unrelated to preference for the insurance and consumption of the insurance, is central to the problem raised by public insurance.[3]

The new equilibrium position of the individual yields different quantities consumed of the goods, due to the addition of the new public service. He can use any quantity of the public insurance and the tax price he pays will not be affected (actually it would be affected, but as one of tens of millions of tax-payers the change would be imperceptible). The individual will spend more of his budget on the public-insurance tax and the consumption good. Because public insurance is a substitute for both private insurance and goods and services designed to reduce the probability of crime, the individual will spend less on A.[4] Figure 6-2 shows the effect on the individual's utility-maximizing position due to the introduction of public insurance.

The budget constraint is shifted downward to account for the tax payment made to support public insurance. For simplicity, although this assumption will be relaxed later, it will be assumed that this individual expects to receive benefits from the program equal to his tax payments. Hence, although he pays tB in taxes, he receives that amount in benefits from public-insurance payments over time, so that his budget remains B. Whether the individual is made better off or

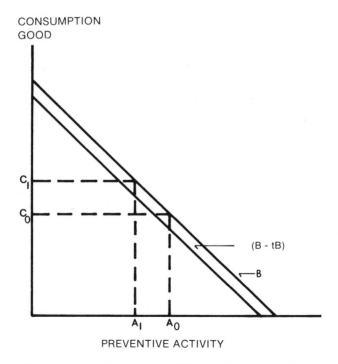

Figure 6-2. Public Insurance Effect on Equilibrium Position

worse off by the program depends on the shape of his indifference function. That is not of concern at this point. The primary effect to be noted is the substitution of public insurance for A. This is the moral-hazard effect.

Expanded Model

Considering the cost of crime to the individual there are two variables to regard: the probability of attack per period and the expected loss per time per period to criminal attack. The probability of crime depends upon the level of protection chosen by the individual. Since the expected loss per period to assault is an environmental constant, once the level of preventive activity is chosen and the probability of attack determined, then the expected loss per period to crime is determined.

In figure 6-3, panel A repeats the commodity space of figures 6-1 and 6-2, where the equilibrium values of the all-purpose commodity and preventive activity are represented. In panel B the relationship between the quantity of preventive activity and the probability of criminal attack is carried over to panel C, which displays the indifference curve for the individual between the two bads he faces, the probability of criminal attack and the expected loss per time period to crime. The individual is indifferent among all positions along curve I. He happens to have p probability of suffering V - L loss in the current time period, but would be willing to trade for more expected loss per period if the probability of criminal attack were reduced. The value of L is exogenous to the individual, but he chooses the value of V and p as best he can, given his budget constraint and preferences.

The positions shown in figure 6-3 are assumed to be the equilibrium values of the variables facing the individual prior to the introduction of public insurance. To understand the impact of public compensation the model has been expanded, as seen in figure 6-4. In this diagram the top two panels have been added to those of figure 6-3. Panel E displays the relationship between the level of public insurance provided to the individual and the expected loss per period to crime. Clearly, the more insurance provided by the state, the lower the expected loss per period for the individual. Panel D illustrates the trade-off between public crime insurance and private activities that is possible when public compensation is available.

The basic change that occurs when the individual moves from his equilibrium position established prior to the introduction of public compensation, as diagramed in figure 6-3, to the new equilibrium he establishes when he adjusts to the existence of the public insurance is shown in figure 6-5. In figure 6-4, the individual was suddenly faced with a new good to use, public insurance. In figure 6-5 he adjusts to the existence of this new good. The shift that occurs in panel A is the same as was discussed for figure 6-2, the substitution of public insurance for private preventive activities, the moral-hazard effect.

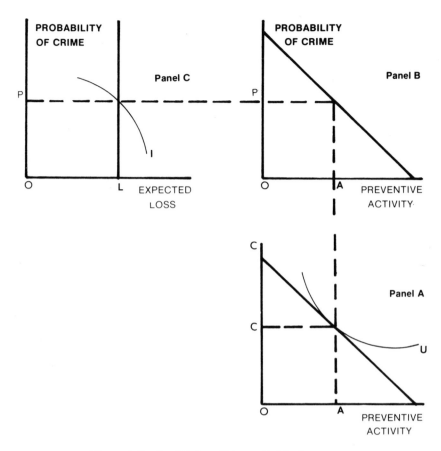

Figure 6–3. Equilibrium Prior to Public Insurance

The decline in equilibrium A causes the probability of criminal attack to increase. This would cause expected losses per period to increase, but the existence of restitution drops the expected loss per period from V - L to V + R - L, so that the new position on the indifference curve I may very well leave the individual no worse off than he was before the public-insurance program existed. As seen in panel D, the existence of public restitution enables the individual to trade preventive activity for restitution payments. Actually the individual is "forced" to use restitution because he cannot choose not to purchase it if he does not like it: all citizens must pay their taxes. He could refuse to accept payments, but it is assumed here that most individuals willl use the program as entitled.

This simple model displays the primary problem presented by public insurance for losses to crime. The problem is the moral-hazard problem, the perverse

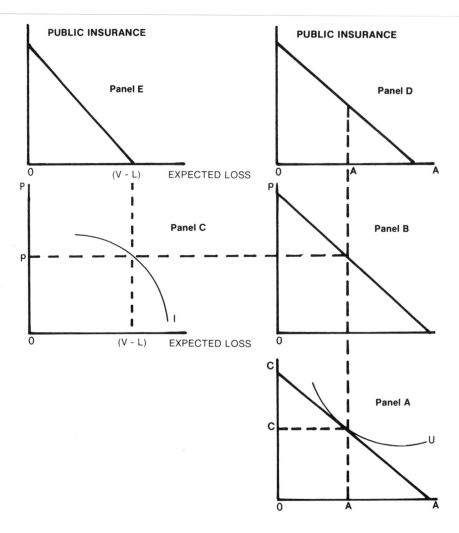

Figure 6–4. Equilibrium Position and Public Insurance

effects on incentives produced by the existence of insurance. Each individual has the incentive to use public insurance as if the price were zero, because his tax "premiums" are unrelated to the benefits he receives from the insurance program. By reducing the amount of preventive activity he purchases, the individual can compensate for the additional losses he will suffer due to criminal attacks with the restitution payments he will receive. As shown in figure 6–5 the individual has adjusted so that he is no worse off than before the program existed. However, the number of criminal attacks has increased.

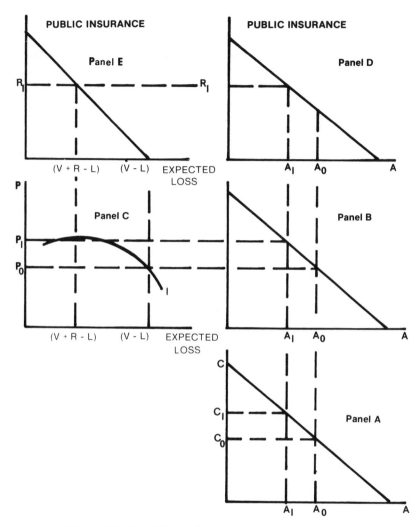

Figure 6-5. Equilibrium Position with Public Insurance

When the increase in crime and its associated resource loss is aggregated for society, the problem becomes more significant. Rather than devoting resources to preventive activity the resources are diverted to pay for the losses caused by the existence of more crime, which is actually a sudsidy for criminal activity. As with most public programs some individuals will be net beneficiaries and others will be net losers, as will be considered shortly. While it is hypothesized here that the public-insurance program would cause a net loss, this cannot be certain unless the hypothesis can be tested.

In some instances collective provision of goods and services is preferable to private provision.[5] It is possible that such is the case for public insurance. An empirical test may become available based on the New Zealand experience with public insurance, which was discussed in chapter two. In accord with the hypothesis here the public insurance would be inefficient, two examples are posited under extremely different assumptions. These situations make extensive use of *ceteris paribus* but may provide some insight into the possible effects of public insurance.

Equal Incomes, Different Preferences. Consider a community divided into three groups of equal size, which differ only in preferences for protection. These three groups are represented by three individuals: Cautious, Daring, and Neutral. Daring, at his present level of income, has no desire to purchase protection but is very much willing to support a public-insurance program for crime victims. The program proposed by Daring will have all individuals paying identical tax shares, because all receive equal incomes and receive full monetary compensation from the public treasury for losses incurred in criminal attacks. Neutral, because he is a sympathetic individual, and because he will receive benefits equal to his tax share, joins Daring in support of the program. It is passed into law by a two-thirds vote over the objection of Cautious, who purchases more preventive activity than either of the other two individuals.

Since the major impacts of the program are on Daring and Cautious, this analysis will consider only what happens to them once the program is implemented. The simple numerical example in table 6-1 will help to illustrate the adjustment process that occurs with the initiation of the public program.

Daring has no use for A at the present price, so he spends his entire income on the all-purpose consumption good. Because of this, Daring has a greater probability of criminal assault each period than does Cautious, who spends 25 units of his income on A. This expenditure reduces the expected loss per period to 10 units for Cautious, compared to 20 units' loss for Daring. These initial private-equilibrium positions are displayed in figure 6-6, which also shows the changes in C and A that occur for both individuals once the public insurance is in effect.

Tax shares for the public-insurance program are the sum of the total losses suffered (which equals restitution) divided by two (ignoring the existence of Neutral, who pays the same as he receives). In the lower part of table 6-1, Daring, who continues to purchase no preventive activity, still loses an average of 20 units per period as before, while Cautious loses an average of 12 units per period to crime, because he purchases less preventive activity than before. The total losses are: 20 + 12 = 32, for a tax share of 16 each, assuming administrative costs to be zero. Cautious incurs higher expected losses to crime because he purchases less A for two reasons: first, he can substitute public insurance for preventive activity, and second, he has suffered a drop in real income because his tax share is larger than his benefits. Daring has incurred an increase in real

Table 6-1
Equal Incomes, Different Preferences

Time Period	Variable	Value per Period Daring	Value per Period Cautious
Prepublic insurance	Gross income	100	100
	Expenditure on A	0	25
	Expected loss to crime	20	10
	Consumption of C	80	65
With public insurance (includes increased crime)	Gross income	100	100
	Expenditure on A	0	20
	Public insurance tax share	16	16
	Expected loss (=restitution)	20	12
	Net value of restitution	+4	−4
	Consumption of C	84	64

income at the expense of Cautious. The net impacts of the program are: a subsidy for Daring's consumption of C at the expense of Cautious, and a subsidy for increased criminal activity. Since Daring has been made better off and Cautious has been made worse off by the program (Neutral remains the same) and there has been a net increase in crime, the overall effect of the program is inefficient.

The inefficient aspects of the public-compensation program in a world of individuals with equal incomes but different preferences is best illustrated in figure 6-5. It displays what happens to Neutral and can be used to consider what happens to Cautious. Both individuals make the same basic shifts in all the quadrants, but Cautious suffers a decline in real income so that for him panel A would be like it is in figure 6-6. The new equilibrium values note the decline in A, which effectively is traded for public insurance. This leads to an increased probability of criminal attack.

Although Cautious expects to lose more to crime, 12 units versus 10 previously, he will be paid for the 12 units he loses by the restitution program, hence his loss falls from V-L to V+R-L. His loss does not fall further because he is not compensated for his nonmonetary losses, such as pain and suffering. The increase in the probability of criminal attack reflects the increase in general criminal activity, which means that more of the society's total resources are being lost to crime.

The program seems to violate fairness in this setting. The initial income equality of the individuals has been destroyed by the subsidy from Cautious to Daring. Cautious has been forced to pay for the losses incurred by a citizen of equal wealth, who happens to have different risk preferences with respect to crime.

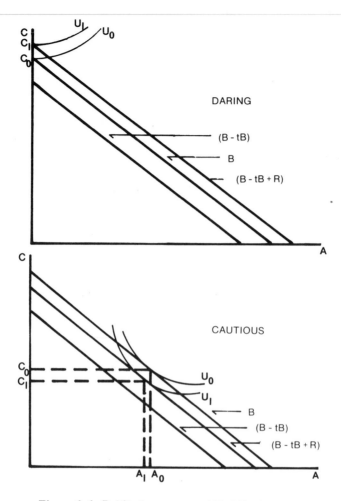

Figure 6–6. Public Insurance and Risk Preferences

Different Incomes, Identical Preferences. Now consider a community composed of three equal-sized groups, represented by Rich, Middle, and Poor, who come from three different income-level groups. However, all individuals have identical preference mappings. Much as in the previous example, assuming that Poor convinces Middle that a public-insurance program is desirable and will cost him nothing, all income transfers will be from Rich to Poor.

This model is closer to the situation envisioned by many proponents of public compensation. They contend that the poor suffer a disproportionately large amount of crime, are least able to protect themselves from crime, and can

least afford to cover the costs crime imposes. The Riches in our society are to subsidize the insurance program for the Poors. This example will indeed be constructed so that Rich does subsidize Poor, so that the good aspect of the program, as advocated by some, can be examined.

For ease of exposition, figure 6-7 places Poor and Rich in commodity spaces drawn to the same scale for comparison purposes. This diagram displays the real-income transfer from Rich to Poor via the public-insurance program. Since Poor receives a subsidy, his real income is increased and he attains a higher level of consumption than before. Rich incurs a loss of real income and consumption.

The final effect of the program here is unclear.[6] The income transfer is accomplished but, due to the substitution of public insurance for A, both may suffer more criminal assaults than in the past. The impact for both would be as in figure 6-5 (except for panel A in figure 6-5). The net effect of the program may be as follows: Rich is left worse off because he loses real income and suffers from more crime; Middle feels no different because the increased crime he suffers is compensated by the public insurance; and Poor is better off because his real income is higher, but he does suffer more criminal attacks. The aggregate impact of the program is to subsidize criminal assaults on individuals of all income levels. This leads to a net loss of resources and is, therefore, inefficient.[7]

The increase in real income received by Poor, the only good or equitable part of the program, for those who view that as a desirable policy goal, could have been accomplished more efficiently, without the side effects on criminal activity. By simply taxing cash from Rich and giving it to Poor, as shown in figure 6-8, the moral-hazard problem is avoided. There is no substitution of public insurance for A. Since C and A are normal goods, as Poor gets more income he will purchase more of both, reducing his chance of criminal assault. Rich would not reduce his consumption of A as much in the case of a cash grant to Poor as when public insurance was the vehicle of the transfer.

Conclusion

Under two sets of extreme assumptions it has been demonstrated that public insurance for the victims of crime is inefficient compared to existing private alternatives. To achieve these results the necessary assumptions had to be strong. The two situations posited would not be easy to test empirically; they are presented as possibilities that may be intuitively plausible. The purpose of the analysis has been to bring forth some considerations about the proposed public-insurance program that have been completely overlooked in all writings on victim compensation.

If the model presented here has validity, then public compensation for pecuniary losses to crime may not generate the benefits intended by the proponents. Economic efficiency is not necessarily the test for a public program.

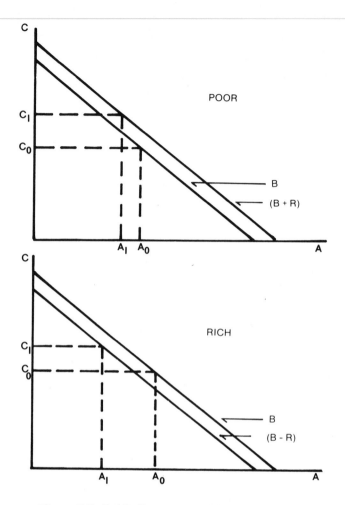

Figure 6-7. Public Insurance and Income Transfers

However, if equity is the primary concern that could lead to the adoption of such a program, then the relative efficiency of alternative methods of providing the desired end should be considered.

Notes

1. See Kenneth J. Arrow, "Uncertainty and the Welfare Economics of Medical Care," *American Economic Review* 53 (1963), pp. 941-73; reprinted in Arrow, *Essays in the Theory of Risk-Bearing* (Chicago: Markham Publishing Co., 1971).

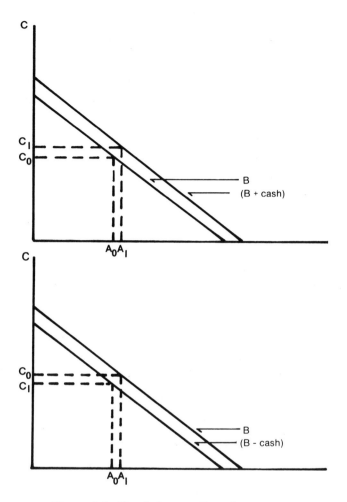

Figure 6–8. Simple Income Transfer

2. However, moral hazard does refer to a situation in which the actions of one person influence the price paid by other parties.

3. It should be noted that it has been assumed that there is interrelationship between private insurance and private goods and services designed to prevent criminal activity. Since they are lumped together as A here, substitution effects can be ignored. Individuals who engage in more preventive activities may pay lower insurance premiums than do individuals who purchase less preventive activity. With respect to crime insurance this effect may not be significant, as claimed by Pauly, but since that effect plays no role here it does not give any unfair advantage to private insurance. See Mark V. Pauly, "Overinsurance and

Public Provision of Insurance: The Roles of Moral Hazard and Adverse Selection" *Quarterly Journal of Economics* 88 (February 1974), p. 48.

4. For any one individual the effect of public insurance on private insurance is not certain. It is possible that they may be complements. If an individual purchased no private insurance prior to the institution of the public insurance, he may now purchase some private insurance to supplement the public insurance. This would probably be the case only for a minority and, in such cases, the insurance may serve as a substitute for the goods and services that reduce the probability of criminal attack, which is the primary trade-off this analysis considers.

5. See James M. Buchanan and Milton Z. Kafoglis, "A Note on Public Goods Supply" *American Economic Review* 53 (June 1963) pp. 403-14.

6. If Rich is victimized more than Poor, there could in fact be a subsidy from Poor to Rich, but here the opposte is assumed.

7. All diagrams have ignored the loss of real income to society as a whole, which would make all individuals considered somewhat worse off than shown.

7

The Relationship of Crime and Punishment and a Concluding Summary

The status of the victims of crime in this country deserves the attention that it is beginning to receive from legislators and scholars. As legal institutions have developed over the past centuries the position of the victim has worsened. Victims have been made almost solely liable for any costs they incur. By itself, victim liability would not yield the tragic results we are experiencing today. The legal position of the victim is essentially the same as it was at the turn of the century. The primary change has been in the status of the criminal, which has led to continual increases in victimization.

Crime and Punishment

Crime is big business in the United States, so the extent of victimization is massive. In 1973 there were approximately 37 million victimizations of persons age twelve and over, households, and businesses.[1] This included 20 million crimes against persons and 15 million crimes against households. Hence, individual citizens suffered the immediate costs of over 35 million crimes (not counting the costs of "victimless crimes," crimes against public property and order, crimes against persons under age twelve, and crimes which occur in relatively small numbers). All categories of crimes have been growing steadily, reported crime doubling in the past decade.[2] There is no evidence of any basic change in this trend.

This should not surprise anyone who believes that punishment deters crime.[3] Over the last three decades fewer and fewer criminals per capita have been sent to prison for committing more and more crime. On a per capita basis, between 1940 and 1970 there was a 30 percent fall in the number of persons sent to prison annually and a similar decline in prison population.[4] Since the cost of committing a crime has declined, the number of profitable crimes has risen. The increase in victimization can be expected as long as this trend continues.[5]

In 1973 there were 204,349 prisoners in state and federal prisons. There were 127,686 commitments from court, parole or conditional-release violators returned, and escapees returned under old sentence. There were 113,771 releases, deaths, and escapes from prison.[6] This means there was an annual turnover of about 120,000 prisoners that year, so that the average sentence served per prisoner was 1.7 years of 600 days.[7] Hence, there were 72 million days served in prison for 1973. Since there were 37 million victimizations in 1973, the

average prison time served per crime was about 2 days.[8] The average time served for murder is much higher than the average time served for burglary and larceny, but it is clear that the expected punishment per crime is lower than many observers believe it to be.

Two interesting points concerning crime have arisen from the data gathered in the victimization surveys. First, the extent of crime is much greater than was known from other reports. Second, the recent increase in crime is not as rapid as has been reported. The number of crimes reported to the police has been widely used as the measure of crime in the United States.[9] Figures since 1940 from the *Uniform Crime Reports* are used here because there are no alternative sources, and because it is assumed that the bias in reporting crime during the time in question did not change, so that the magnitudes of the changes in crime over time are useful.[10]

Table 7-1 displays the traditional *Uniform Crime Reports* crime index with larceny excluded. Because the dollar definition of larceny has changed over time and because inflation biases upward the number of $50 minimum larcenies over time, that crime is subtracted from the index.[11] Table 7-2 displays the percentage increase in crime during the last several decades. The inflationary bias to the index caused by the normal dollar definition of larceny is illustrated there.[12]

The estimate of the magnitude of crime and the rate of increase in crime can now be compared to one estimate of the punishment for crime in the same time period. Table 7-3 shows the index of reported crime less larceny and the number of individuals received by the prisons from the courts per 100,000 civilian population. The crime index is then divided by the prisoner index to display the number of crimes reported in each year per individual sentenced to prison.

The change in the magnitude of the number of crimes committed for every criminal sent to prison is the factor to be noted. By 1974 there were six times as

Table 7-1
Reported Crime in the United States[a]

| | Number | | Index[b] | |
Year	All	All Less Larceny	All	All Less Larceny
1940	677,844	620,464	514.8	471.2
1950	988,114	745,869	655.7	494.9
1960	2,019,600	1,512,300	1,126.2	843.9
1970	5,581,200	3,831,400	2,746.9	1,885.7
1974	10,192,034	4,964,338	4,821.4	2,348.4

Source: *Uniform Crime Reports.*

[a]Includes homicide, rape, robbery, burglary, larceny, and motor vehicle theft, reported to the police.

[b]Per 100,000 population.

Table 7-2
Percent Increase in Reported Crime Index

Time Period	All	All Larceny
1940–50	27.37	5.03
1950–60	71.76	70.40
1960–70	143.91	123.61
1970–74	75.52	24.54
1940–70	433.59	300.19
1940–74	836.56	398.39

Source: Same as table 7-1.

Table 7-3
Reported Crimes per Sentenced Prisoner[a]

Year	Crime Index	Prisoner Index	Crimes/Prisoner
1940	471.2	55.5	8.49
1950	494.9	46.1	10.74
1960	843.3	49.3	17.11
1970	1,885.7	39.0	48.35
1974	2,348.4	49.4	47.54

Source: Same as table 7-1. Prisoner data from *Sourcebook of Criminal Justice Statistics 1973*, pp. 346, 359; *Sourcebook of Criminal Justice Statistics 1976*, p. 398.

[a]Per 100,000 population.

many crimes committed for every one person sentenced to prison than in 1940. Since the length of sentences served has not changed significantly over the years, the 1974 figure could be viewed as a reduction in punishment for crimes to one-sixth of the 1940 level.[13]

The actual ratio of crimes committed per individual sentenced can be estimated for 1973. For all 37 million victimizations (not just reported crimes), which excludes millions of victimless crimes, approximately 120,000 persons were sentenced to prison or returned to prison for violating parole or conditional release.[14] This means there were about 300 victimization incidents for every one person admitted to prison that year. For the violent crimes of rape, robbery, and aggravated assault there were approximately 82 crimes for every one criminal admitted to prison for those offenses. For burglary the ratio of crimes committed per prisoner admitted was about 315 to 1. For property crimes the ratios are even larger, but are not accurate due to the number of individuals who serve short jail terms for those crimes, for which data are not available.[15]

Two conclusions may be drawn from the numbers presented here. First, the punishment per crime seems low. Second, the odds of a criminal being sent to prison for any one criminal act are low. These factors are often listed

as two of the major deterrents to crime. Yet, for crimes that often inflict large monetary, physical, and psychological costs on victims, the punishment appears, to this observer, to be very low.

The chance of punishment and the extent of punishment are only two of the factors to be considered by a criminal. The income from crime is another factor. Evidence about the income of criminals from crime is scarce. However, given the large number of crimes, it clearly is an activity that has become more desirable to more individuals.

Unfortunately little is known of the incomes of professional or part-time criminals. One researcher, by interviewing many criminals, was able to estimate the annual income of successful criminals. These individuals specialized in particular crimes and received the following incomes, tax free, in the first half of the 1970s: hotel burglar, $75,000; pickpocket, $20,000; house burglar, $25,000; industrial burglar, $75,000; shoplifter, $15,000; hit man, $75,000; bank robber, $24,000; drug importer, $165,000; and securities thief, $100,000.[16] These figures are not necessarily representative of the income earned by all criminals, but give some evidence of how people can live by crime. Since the benefits from criminal activity appear to be substantial, at least for some individuals, and the expected punishment per crime committed is quite low, it does not seem surprising that there is a large amount of criminal activity.

Three interesting points concerning crime have arisen from the data gathered in the victimization surveys. First, the extent of crime is much greater than was known from other reports. Second, the recent increase in crime is not as rapid as has been reported. Third, some cities have an unfair reputation as "crime capitals." The number of crimes reported to the police, estimated by the *Uniform Crime Reports,* has been widely used as the measure of crime in the United States. As shown in table 7–4, reported crimes are only a fraction of the victimizations that occur, according to the victimization surveys.

Although the number of crimes that occur is much higher than the numbers usually publicized, the increase in victimizations, at least for 1973 to 1974, is not as high as reported crimes. Why the number of reported crimes should have increased so much more than the number of victimizations is not clear. Several explanations have been offered for this occurrence, which is illustrated by table 7–5. It is possible that the publication of the victimization surveys pressured police departments to increase reported crimes so there would not be as large a difference between reported and actual crime. It is also possible that large increases are reported to make an effective case for continued budget increase for police departments, at a time when many governments were not experiencing revenue increases as large as in prior years. Neither of the arguments may be entirely correct, but it has not been demonstrated why individual victims would have had a greater incentive to report crimes in 1974 than in 1973.

When the *Uniform Crime Reports* are issued every year, newspapers frequently use the figures listed there to see how their city stands with respect to crime. This has led to an unfair and unfounded characterization of some cities

Table 7–4
Reported Crimes as a Percent of Victimizations[a] (1973)

Category	Victimizations	Reported Crimes	Reported Crime per Victimization
Violent Crimes	3,232,758	871,450	.27
Aggravated Assault	1,687,254	417,430	.25
Robbery	1,383,268	383,260	.28
Rape	162,236	51,230	.32
Property Crimes	31,894,148	7,794,800	.24
Burglary	7,820,579	2,549,900	.33
Larceny	22,740,667	4,319,100	.19
Motor Vehicle Theft	1,332,902	925,700	.69

Source: Reported crimes from *Uniform Crime Reports–1974*, p. 55, are based on a 1973 population of 209,851,000. Murder and manslaughter were excluded here because they were not covered by the victimization survey (19,350 were reported). Victimizations from *Criminal Victimization in the United States–1973 Advance Report*, pp. 12, 19, 23, are based on a 1973 population of 162,236,000 (persons age 12 and over), a household population of 69,442,000, and a business establishment population of 6,800,000.

[a]The figures are not completely comparable due to a small difference in the population base and due to possible differences in the understanding of what constituted a particular crime, but this does not appear to have been a major problem.

Table 7–5
Percent Change in Reported Crimes and Victimizations[a] (1973–74)[a]

Category	Reported Crimes	Victimizations	Difference
Aggravated Assault	+8.0	+3.3	4.7
Robbery	+14.5	+6.1	8.4
Rape	+7.4	+4.3	3.1
Burglary	+18.0	+2.1	15.9
Larceny	+20.6	+7.1	12.9
Motor Vehicle Theft	+4.7	−1.7	6.4

Source: *Uniform Crime Reports–1973, 1974*, pp. 58 and 55, respectively; *Criminal Victimization in the United States–A Comparison of 1973 and 1974 Findings*, pp. 11, 24, 33.

[a]For victimizations the robbery, burglary, and larceny figures are weighted averages of the averages reported for personal crimes, household crimes, and business crimes, where appropriate. A similar difference is found when comparing the change in reported crime and victimizations in years 1974–1975.

as "crime capitals," while others are pictured as having relatively little crime. In fact the opposite may sometimes be the case. As seen in table 7-6, according to the 1973 *Uniform Crime Reports* index of violent crimes, New York and Miami stand out as cities with above average crime. However, an examination of the victimization index of personal crimes of violence reveals those same cities to be below average with respect to victimizations.

Table 7–6
Indexes of Crimes of Violence^a (1973)

City	Reported Crime Index	Victimization Index
Atlanta	6.2	32
Baltimore	9.2	49
Boston	4.1	49
Buffalo	3.0	32
Chicago	7.3	42
Cincinnati	2.8	38
Cleveland	4.5	45
Dallas	5.0	29
Denver	5.2	42
Detroit	8.2	53
Houston	5.0	37
Los Angeles	8.4	23
Miami	9.5	17
Milwaukee	1.7	37
Minneapolis	3.0	42
Newark	5.5	34
New Orleans	6.6	33
New York	12.0	29
Philadelphia	4.4	46
Pittsburgh	2.8	30
Portland	1.7	38
St. Louis	6.0	32
San Diego	3.1	29
San Francisco	6.8	46
Washington, D.C.	6.4	24

Source: *Sourcebook of Criminal Justice Statistics–1975,* pp. 252–65; *Criminal Victimization Surveys in 13 American Cities; Criminal Victimization Surveys in the Nation's Five Largest Cities; Criminal Victimization Surveys in Eight American Cities.*

^{a}Per 100,000 population. The Reported Crime Index, from the *Uniform Crime Reports,* includes: murder, rape, aggravated assault and robbery. The Victimization Index, from LEAA victimization surveys, includes: rape, aggravated assault, and robbery. The victimization surveys for Chicago, Detroit, Los Angeles, New York, and Philadelphia were taken in 1972. The victimization surveys for Atlanta, Baltimore, Cleveland, Dallas, Denver, Newark, Portland, and St. Louis were taken in 1971/72 and 1974/75; the average of those two surveys was taken for the 1973 index.

The two crime indexes are not optimal for comparison. The *Uniform Crime Reports* index is for the standard metropolitan statistical area (SMSA) of the cities in question. The LEAA victimization surveys were taken in the cities themselves. Hence, the population bases of the two surveys differ in size and income and racial composition, since the cities are generally central cities, while the SMSAs include the suburbs. However, it does appear that there is a greater tendency for the citizens in some cities to report crimes to the police than there is in other cities. New York and Miami appear to be "crime capitals" because the residents of those cities may report more victimization incidents to the

police than do the residents of Milwaukee, Minneapolis, and Portland. It is not clear why the residents of some cities report more crimes to the police than do the residents of other cities. It is possible that in certain cities the residents believe that their police departments are quite efficient, so that calling the police is "worthwhile" when a victimization occurs. One can suggest other reasons based on demographic and sociological grounds, but further study should be required before generalizations are made. Although it must be emphasized that these indexes are not on identical bases, there seems to be good reason to doubt the usefulness of the *Uniform Crime Reports* as a measure of the extent of crime in American cities.

Is Victim Compensation the Answer?

If there is a lack of will on the part of the political and the judicial system to deal severely with criminals, victimization will continue to be a tragic problem, so long as the punishment per crime is as low as it is at present. It now costs victims tens of billions of dollars annually, and will grow worse as the value of crime increases. There appears to be no substantive judicial or political move to lessen the costs of victimization by instituting actions that would reduce the number of crimes committed.

Victim compensation is an attempt to lighten some of the immediate costs of victimization suffered by some individuals. It would, of course, do nothing to reduce the gross costs of victimization. Indeed, one point of this book has been to demonstrate that, at the very least, compensation would result in more resources being devoted to the area of victimization, even if the volume of crime were unaffected. As now designed, victim compensation could make the number of victimizations increase—certainly the opposite of the result desired by anyone other than a professional criminal.

The only way that the costs of victimization can be reduced, and the plight of the victims of crime significantly bettered, is for the root of the problem to be attacked, not by masking the problem with political placebos, which could burgeon into tax burdens in the future. As noted in congressional testimony, if victim compensation "should become perverted into a syndrome whereby the criminal is, in effect, *subsidized* by the state then a terrible disservice will have been done to the safety of society." If compensation is to be adopted, "the criminal justice system must still bend every effort to prevent crime from happening in the first place."[17]

Charitably, victim compensation, as now proposed, can be viewed as an imperfect humanitarian attempt to do something beneficial for truly unfortunate people. At worst it can be viewed as a subsidy for lawyers, another layer of bureaucracy, and an attempt to sooth public ire toward public officials and members of the judiciary who did much to create the terrible problem we have

today. A political palliative may retard the day when the pressures for strong actions against criminals build to the point where politicians are forced to pass measures designed to stop criminals. In the meantime the position of individuals as victims would have continued to worsen.

In chapter two, a review of historical evidence indicated that most societies relied upon restitution by the criminal until the state decided to punish criminals, casting aside the victims. In some cases, when the criminal did not compensate his victim, the neighbors of the victim were forced to pay for the damages done. This served as a form of insurance, and as an incentive for individuals to provide protection via vigilance in their own community. These different forms of legal organizations, by imposing restitution and/or severe punishments, provided various incentives to reduce crime.

The compensation employed today in many jurisdictions, and proposed for the entire nation, provides no incentives to prevent crime. Since the compensation is made from a tax paid by tens of millions, no one individual will feel any incentive to be more vigilant in preventing crimes in hopes of reducing his compensation contribution. Some scholars have said that we should look to history for examples of "enlightened" societies which provided for the victims of crime. Indeed we should. The lesson learned is that no society ever employed a compensation system like the one proposed now. One would not expect developing societies to allow irrational institutions to emerge and exist, if the societies were to be successful.

One reason irrational institutions can emerge and persist is because of the nature of certain political institutions. As discussed in chapter four, the primary forces pushing for adoption of public compensation are special-interest groups which will benefit from the existence of such a program. There is no lobby of past or potential victims arguing for implementation of public restitution. The direct pressure is from lawyers, bureaucrats, and other groups which perceive benefits from the legislation. There is little evidence that purely humanitarian interests have ever generated such programs.

Political gains to politicians from special interests and some general popular interest in public compensation may lead to adoption of the program. Bureaucratic interests would cause the program to expand in size and function. The use of a 50 percent matching grant to finance the state programs would insure growth of the program, much more than if states had to finance the programs individually or if a compensation program were only at the federal level. Since the decision cost to the states would be only one-half of what they would spend, and since the federal government would be bound to pay for whatever the states spend, the program would seem likely to grow rapidly. Program administrators and laywers are given a good opportunity to expand the program beyond its present intent, and it is to be expected that they will take advantage of their opportunities.

Individuals favoring state-sponsored restitution may see nothing wrong with the expansion of the program to the size estimated in chapter four. However, if justice for victims is truly desired, and humanitarian notions are to prevail, then the proposed program should be equitable. In a democratic setting, Rawlsian notions of justice appear to provide a proper perspective. However, as discussed in chapter five, the application of such a paradigm of justice does not appear to generate a compensation program of the nature of the one considered here. In a constitutional setting, fairness would dictate that the criminal be liable for the costs suffered by victims. In an operational contractual setting, where many victims continue to suffer despite the liability of the criminals, justice may dictate aid for victims. Basic justice would dictate that equal victims be treated as equals. Vertical and horizontal equity is called for, not some notion of justice according to income at the time of victimization.

A program designed to be just and to provide equal treatment for equal victims would also be based on some criterion of efficiency. Chapter six points out that if two potential programs are of equal justice, one would rationally choose the program with greater economic efficiency. The current programs and the proposed national program meet neither tests of equity nor efficiency. Even if the current program were changed to treat equals as equals, it would fail on the grounds of economic efficiency, in comparison to the alternatives discussed previously, which would make use of co-insurance and other features to help reduce the moral-hazard problem.

It may be that this society has fallen into what James Buchanan has called the samaritan's dilemma.[18] That is, there may have been basic changes in behavioral standards. If there has been a collective loss of will to enforce the laws and punish those who break the laws, the situation may never be reversed. Victim compensation seems to be a part of the perverse collective response to the ogre of crime, with which we seem unable to deal despite general agreement on the basic solution. It may be trite to say that we can learn from history, but Sir Henry Maine, citing the lack of will in ancient Rome to enforce the law and the disorder which resulted, contended: "No cause contributed so powerfully to the decay of political capacity in the Roman people as this periodic abeyance of the laws; and, when it had once been resorted to, we need not hesitate to assert that the ruin of Roman liberty became merely a question of time."[19]

Notes

1. U.S., National Criminal Justice Information and Statistics Service, *Criminal Victimization in the United States*, a National Crime Panel Survey Report, no. SC-NCP-N-2 (Washington, D.C.: U.S.G.P.O., 1975), p. 1.

2. According to the estimates and figures provided in the FBI's annual *Uniform Crime Reports*.

3. After a long period of disfavor by intellectuals, the belief that punishment does deter crime is being revived in academia. See Marc F. Plattner, "The Rehabilitation of Punishment," *Public Interest* 44 (Summer 1976), pp. 104–14.

4. U.S., National Criminal Justice Information and Statistics Service, *Sourcebook of Criminal Justice–1973*, Michael J. Hindeland et al., eds. (Washington, D.C.: U.S.G.P.O., 1974), pp. 346, 350.

5. For the fundamental analysis of crime activity, see Gordon Tullock, *The Logic of the Law* (New York: Basic Books, 1971); and Gary S. Becker, "Crime and Punishment: An Economic Approach," *Journal of Political Economy* 76 (March 1968):169-218.

6. U.S., National Criminal Justice Information and Statistics Service, *Prisoners in State and Federal Institutions on December 31, 1971, 1972, 1973,* National Prisoner Statistics Bulletin no. SD-NPS-PSF-1 (Washington, D.C.: U.S.G.P.O., 1975), pp. 12, 12, 25.

7. This estimate is backed by several other sources. See *Sourcebook of Criminal Justice Statistics–1973,* pp. 381–419.

8. This figure may be contested but it is believed by the author to be accurate. The prison man-days are biased upward by time served for homicide, drug law violations, and other crimes not counted in the victimizations. These crimes appear to comprise over 10 percent of the violations for which time in prison is served. The population of the nation's local jails was about 140,000 in 1973. This figure was excluded because most jail inmates are awaiting legal action. Those serving time are often there for offenses not included in the victimization totals. In 1973 there were 1.6 million arrests for drunkenness, 1 million arrests for driving under the influence, .7 million arrests for disorderly conduct, .6 million arrests for drug law violations, .4 million arrests for simple assault, and arrests for prostitution and other nonvictim offenses. See U.S., National Justice Information and Statistics Service, *The Nation's Jails,* report no. SD-J-4 (Washington, D.C.: U.S.G.P.O., 1975), p. 23; Federal Bureau of Investigation, *Crime in the United States,* Uniform Crime Reports 1973 (Washington, D.C.: U.S.G.P.O., 1974), p. 121; *Sourcebook of Criminal Justice Statistics–1973,* pp. 363, 381–415.

9. For many years the FBI's *Uniform Crime Reports* were the best sources of information, and often the only sources, for many topics in the area of criminal activity.

10. There are arguments on both sides of the incentive to deflate or inflate reported crime, but no convincing argument has been made, except for the immediate past, as to which trend predominated.

11. The crimes included in the index are: murder, rape, aggravated assault, burglary, robbery, and auto theft.

12. It is possible, of course, that larceny has increased at a greater rate than the rest of the crimes in the index, but inflation has undoubtedly biased the counting of larceny. Using the consumer price index, with 1957 as the base for

$50, the equivalent nominal dollar values are: 1940, $24.9; 1950, $42.8; 1960, $52.6; 1970, $68.9; and 1974, $87.6.

13. Remember that the crimes included in the crime index comprise only a fraction of the crimes committed, while the prisoner index includes all individuals sentenced by state and federal courts.

14. Approximately 15 or 20 percent of those in prisons in 1973 were there for victimless crimes, such as: drug offenses, weapons offenses, drunk or drugged driving, escape or flight, and jail offenses. These prisoners are left in the total number admitted to prison because the total cannot be accurately broken down by reason for admission in 1973. In any event the basic result is not changed. See U.S., National Criminal Justice Information and Statistics Service, *Survey of Inmates of State Correctional Facilities—1974 Annual Report,* National Prisoner Statistics Special Report no. SD–NPS–SR–2 (Washington, D.C.: U.S.G.P.O., March 1976), p. 28.

15. For motor-vehicle thefts the ratio was 278 to 1; for larceny the ratio was almost 3,000 to 1. These ratios would be affected by jail sentences, but the larceny ratio would still be very large. These ratios were based on the assumption that 60 percent of the prisoners in prison in January 1974 were there for crimes committed in 1973, based on the annual admission and departure rate. The ratios shown are not accurate but appear to be generally correct.

16. Thomas Plate, *Crime Pays!* (New York: Simon and Schuster, 1975), p. 92.

17. Testimony of Frank Carrington, Executive Director, Americans for Effective Law Enforcement, Inc., U.S., House, Committee on the Judiciary, *Crime Victim Compensation,* Hearings, 94th Cong., 1975 and 1976, serial no. 39, p. 513.

18. James M. Buchanan, "The Samaritan's Dilemma," in *Altruism, Morality, and Economic Theory,* Edmund Phelps, ed. (New York: Russell Sage Foundation, 1975), pp. 71–86.

19. Henry S. Maine, *Ancient Law* (London: John Murray, 11th ed., 1887), p. 390.

Appendix A:
Prison Labor Restrictions

The prison labor sector has gone from indentured servitude, to competitive contracting for labor, to state-directed production, to an almost absolute limit on labor. The collective power of organized labor to influence markets via the legislative process is illustrated, as is the relative efficiency of markets organized in different manners.

This appendix will give cursory treatment to some prison labor history, but will cover the basic developments, so that the richness of the history can be appreciated. Some parts of prison labor history will be developed more fully. A few economic implications and explanations will be provided.

In American history there have been several different systems of prisoner labor used. They are categorized by one author as: public account, contract, piece-price, lease, state-use, and public works.[1] The last two systems are essentially the same: prisoners are assigned to work on some public project either in or out of the prison system. This system is common today for the small amount of labor done by prisoners. The piece-price system can be considered to be a variation on the contract system, which will be discussed in detail.

The lease system was used, in colonial America, as a form of indentured servitude. Prisoners were usually bid for competitively, and went for the highest price. The system was also widely used in the South for leasing large gangs of prisoners to work on various private projects. The public-account system is a prison industry run by the state, usually as a part of the prison system. This is still in use today, but is limited in scope. The contract system was the most important system before the twentieth century. Private parties would bid for the use of convict labor in private factories located near or in the prison.

In seventeenth- and eighteenth-century America, jails were generally a local operation. Most jails either leased the prisoners into the custody of the highest bidder, so that funds could be raised to pay restitution to his victim, or the individual was left to work in jail. Family members or another individual could provide the prisoner with the tools necessary to work at some craft, so that funds could be raised to cover the expenses of the jailing. This system was in disfavor with some religious sects, such as the Quakers in Pennsylvania, and was terminated when states began to establish state prisons about the start of the nineteenth century.

Different states employed different systems of labor for the prisoners. Most common were the public-account system and the contract system. The simultaneous operation enabled the states to compare performance of the different systems. The goods produced under either system could be sold in the market in competition with all products produced by free labor. The differences between the two systems were illustrated by the following comments:

... the public account system proved economically unsatisfactory. The products were inferior in quality to those of free labor, commanded a small and inadequate market, and yielded so small an income to the prison authorities as to incur a chronic deficit in the management of the prison industries.[2]

In contrast, the contract system, which usually produced labor contracts from five to ten years in duration, was cited for the following advantages:

1. Under it, convicts are much more regularly employed, as the contractors are much abler business men than the prison wardens. 2. It is very remunerative to the state. The institutions which employ this system are able to realize sums equal to 65 per cent of their current expenses. . . . [3]

Despite the economic advantages to the contract system, prison officials resisted its introduction, preferring the public-account system, which gave them control of production. However, by the 1820s and 1830s the contract system was established in most states. By the mid-1800s the system was almost universal in use in the United States. As a result of the system prison managers "wiped out the deficits in the prison industries and began to produce a net income."[4]

The trade unions of the 1820s protested the competition posed by prison labor. New York cabinetmakers wanted the prisoners to stop producing cabinets and instead work in a state marble quarry.[5] These protests were as ineffective as were the unions themselves, and died, as did the unions, until after the Civil War. By the 1880s renewed attacks on the contract system began to take a toll. States began to revert back to the public-account system and to use more public works to occupy the prisoners. In 1886 the Knights of Labor "demanded that the states enact laws for the branding of prison goods, that the hours of labor for convicts be shortened to six . . . and that no convicts be employed on government works."[6] The protest of labor, which was couched in terms of benefits for the prisoners, was joined by the manufacturers of goods in competition with those produced by contract prison labor. A group of these manufacturers met in Chicago in 1886 and formed the National Anti-Convict Contract Association.[7] They pushed for federal legislation to prohibit the sale of any convict-made goods in interstate commerce.

Despite the protests, the volume of convict-made goods was never very large. An 1887 study by the Commissioner of Labor "showed that the products of prisons composed but .54 per cent of the total mechanical products of the country."[8] However, it noted that in certain markets the competition was significant. A study of the cooperage market in Chicago from 1875–85 revealed that prison contractors furnished 67.8 percent of the total product, and that there was a 360 percent increase in volume during that time.[9] The wages of free laborers in that market fell by 30 percent in those years (apparently the general price level was falling during that time).

The decline of the use of the contract system, and the resulting decline in the output ability of prison industry, is demonstrated by table A-1 from a study by the Commissioner of Labor. The contract system fell into disfavor in the states and was finally killed by the federal government. The lease system was outlawed a few years before the contract system. It had been used primarily in the Southern states after the Civil War. It used mostly black convicts and was tainted by political payoffs and great cruelty. Federal legislation in the early 1900s ended the leasing system, but convicts could still be used in gang-type work, so long as done for a government project.

In 1929 Congress enacted the Hawes-Cooper Act. It provided that, effective January 19, 1934, "All goods . . . produced . . . by convicts . . . shall upon arrival and delivery [in a state] be subject to the operation and effect of the laws of [the state] to the same extent and in the same manner as though such goods . . . had been manufactured . . . in such State. . . ."[10] By this statute states were empowered to pass legislation prohibiting the sale of convict-made goods on the open market, despite the fact that the goods were in interstate commerce. By 1933, due to lobbying efforts of such groups as the AFL, nineteen states had adopted such statutes.[11] The AFL only opposed the sale of convict-made goods on the open market. It did not oppose the sale of such goods to state governments.

The Ashurst-Sumners Act was adopted by Congress in 1935. Strengthened by another act in 1940, it now provides: "Whoever . . . transports in interstate commerce . . . any goods . . . produced . . . wholly or in part by convicts . . . shall be fined not more than $1,000 or imprisoned not more than one year, or both."[12] It also requires prisoner-made goods in interstate commerce "shall be plainly and clearly marked" as to origin.[13]

Intrastate commerce in prisoner-made goods is barred in most states. For example, in Florida the law allows for public-account prison industry.[14] However,

Table A-1

Summary of Value of Goods Produced or Work Done by Systems of Work, 1885 and 1895

(value in dollars)

	Value	
Systems of Work	1885	1895
Public Account System	2,063,892.18	4,888,563.36
Contract System	17,071,265.67	8,190,799.70
Piece-price System	1,484,230.52	3,795,483.24
Lease System	3,651,690.00	2,167,626.03
Totals	24,271,078.37	19,042,472.33

Source: Henry C. Mohler, "Convict Labor Policies," *Journal of Criminal Law and Criminology* 51 (1925), p. 579.

the goods produced may not be sold in the open market. They can be sold only to state agencies. Similarly, prisoners can be used for work outside of the prison, but only in public works for state agencies. A limited number of goods may be produced for sale to local governments, such as furniture, farm products, and janitorial supplies.

Federal prisons are subject to numerous restrictions on federal prisoners' labor. Federal Prison Industries is a government corporation which utilizes inmate labor to make such items as canvas duffel bags and mailbags, brushes, metal furniture, and mattresses. The goods can be produced only for sale to federal agencies. The items produced must be diverse so "that no single private industry shall be forced to bear an undue burden of competition from the products of the prison workshops, and to reduce to a minimum competition with private industry or free labor."[15] Various statutes provide that convict labor cannot be used in federally financed highway construction, in federal airport development projects, in the production of equipment to be used by the U.S. Postal Service, or in the production of materials to be supplied to the government under a contract of more than $10,000.[16]

The result of these legal restrictions is that in the states, "the vast majority of the approximately 220,000 inmates of our penitentiaries at present have very little work to keep them occupied other than housekeeping and maintenance duties."[17] In the federal prison system, which has a better-developed industrial program, "only about thirty percent of the inmate population is employed in industry."[18] As a result, most prisoners have very light duties; most of their time is idle. In 1967, only about one-quarter of all federal prison inmates were employed by Federal Prison Industries. They were paid an average of $494 per year, in the production of $58.3 million worth of goods.[19]

Opposition to prison labor, which appears to have had a negative impact on the usefulness of prisons, was based on misconceptions about the potential advantages to limiting prison-labor production. The gains to the firms and unions which fought for the labor restrictions were very small. In the long run, it may well be that the trivial increment to free-labor wages is outweighed by the negative impact of nonproductive prison labor.[20] Nonproducing prisoners must be supported by taxes paid by free labor. There is no longer a significant chance for prisoners to earn money to pay restitution to the victims of crime. The crime rate as a whole may be increased by the lack of useful skills learned and held by prisoners, who in turn may be more likely to find crime more profitable than labor after leaving prison than they would if they worked at productive positions while incarcerated.

Notes

1. Henry C. Mohler, "Convict Labor Policies," *Journal of Criminal Law and Criminology* 15 (1925), p. 530.

2. Ibid., p. 557.

3. Ibid., p. 550.

4. Ibid., p. 559.

5. Gill, "The Prison Labor Problem," 157 *Annals* 83 (1931).

6. Mohler, "Convict Labor Policies," p. 569.

7. Ibid., p. 570.

8. Ibid., pp. 570-71.

9. Ibid.

10. 49 *U.S.C.,* §60.

11. B. Jacob, "Reparation or Restitution by the Criminal Offender to His Victim," *J. Crim. Law and Criminology* 61 (1970), p. 158.

12. 18 *U.S.C.,* §1761.

13. 18 *U.S.C.,* §1762.

14. *Florida Statutes,* §§945.06-945.16 (1975).

15. 18 *U.S.C.,* §4122(b).

16. Jacob, "Reparation or Restitution," p. 159.

17. Ibid., p. 160.

18. Ibid.

19. Ibid.

20. Ibid., pp. 160-61.

Appendix B:
Niskanen's Model of
Bureaucracy

Niskanen's model of bureaucratic supply of public output assumes the relation between a bureau and its sponsor is that of a bilateral monopoly.[1] A federal bureau is the sole supplier of a certain set of activities to a single sponsor, usually Congress. Given the relative incentives and available information, the bureau has dominant monopoly power. To maximize utility and to survive the competition for funds, Niskanen hypothesizes that bureaucrats seek to maximize the size of the budget under their control.

The marginal valuation (demand) curve, CE, in figure A-1 represents the sponsor's preferences. If the preferences of the sponsors reflect the preferences of all citizens, CE portrays the sum of the citizens' marginal valuations of the bureau's services. The constraint on the bureau is that the total costs of supplying the service must not be greater than the available budget. The equilibrium rate of output is the point where the marginal valuation of output is zero, point E. The equilibrium budget equals the area under the marginal-valuation curve, unless the minimum cost of that output is greater than the maximum budget

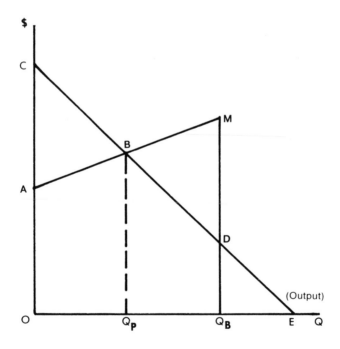

Figure B-1. Niskanen's Basic Model of Bureaucracy

(OCE). If so, the bureau is budget-constrained. Then the equilibrium rate of output is where total cost (the area under the marginal-cost curve, AM) and total budget are equal. As shown in figure A-1 the equilibrium budget is Q_B. The budget is $OAMO_B$ (= $OCDQ_B$).

Breton and Wintrobe contend that the output that will emerge will lie somewhere between Q_P and Q_B. The bureau will strive to achieve Q_B with budget $OCDQ_B$. The sponsoring politicians are motivated to supply public goods to where the sum of the marginal benefits to the citizens equals the marginal cost of supplying that good. Hence, the politicians desire Q_P supplied at minimum cost, yielding budget $OABQ_P$. The difference between the two budgets (ACB) is the amount of consumers' surplus appropriated by the bureau.

Under this modified Niskanen model, politicians will use control devices, which are costly, to help reduce excess budgets of bureaus. The sponsors will incur control expenditures up to the point at which the marginal benefits of such controls are equal to the marginal costs of the controls. The output and budget that emerges will depend upon the costliness of the control devices. The greater the costs in comparison to the benefits, the higher the budget.

Note

1. This summary is drawn from: Albert Breton and Ronald Wintrobe, "The Equilibrium Size of a Budget-Maximizing Bureau," *Journal of Political Economy* 83 (February 1975), pp. 195–207; and William Niskanen, *Bureaucracy and Representative Government* (Chicago: Aldine, 1971), ch. 3.

Bibliography

Articles

Alchian, Armen, and Demsetz, Harold. "Production, Information Costs, and Economic Organization." *American Economic Review* 62 (December 1972): 777-95.

Alexander, Sidney S. "Social Evaluation Through Notional Choice." *Quarterly Journal of Economics* 88 (November 1974): 597-624.

Arrow, Kenneth J. "Uncertainty and the Welfare Economics of Medical Care." *American Economic Review* 53 (1963): 941-73.

Becker, Gary S. "Crime and Punishment: An Economic Approach." *Journal of Political Economy* 76 (March 1968): 169-218.

_____, and Ehrlich, Isaac. "Market Insurance, Self-Insurance, and Self-Protection." *Journal of Political Economy* 80 (July 1972): 623-48.

Breton, Albert, and Wintrobe Ronald. "The Equilibrium Size of a Budget-Maximizing Bureau." *Journal of Political Economy* 83 (February 1975): 195-207.

Brett, Peter. "Compensation for the Victims of Crime: New Zealand's Pioneering Statute." *Australian Lawyer* 5 (1964): 21-27.

Buchanan, James M. "A Hobbesian Interpretation of the Rawlsian Difference Principle." *Kyklos* 29 (1976): 5-25.

_____. "The Inconsistencies of the National Health Service." Institute of Economic Affairs, *Occasional Papers,* no. 7 (November 1965).

_____. "The Samaritan's Dilemma." In *Altruism, Morality, and Economic Theory,* edited by Edmund S. Phelps, pp. 71-86. New York: Russell Sage Foundation, 1975.

_____, and Bush, Winston. "Political Constraints on Contractual Redistribution." *American Economic Review* 64 (May 1974): 153-57.

_____, and Kafoglis, Milton Z. "A Note on Public Goods Supply." *American Economic Review* 53 (June 1963): 403-14.

Burns, Peter, and Ross, Alan M. "A Comparative Study of Victims of Crime Indemnification in Canada." *University of British Columbia Law Review* 8 (1973): 105-35.

Chappell, Duncan. "Compensating Australian Victims of Violent Crime." *Australian Law Journal* 41 (1967): 3-11.

_____. "The Emergence of Australian Schemes to Compensate Victims of Crime." *Southern California Law Review* 43 (1970): 69-83.

Childress, Robert D. "Compensation for Criminally Inflicted Personal Injury." *New York University Law Review* 39 (1964): 444-71.

Cosway, Richard. "Crime Compensation." *Washington Law Review* 49 (1974): 551-70.

111

Covey, Joan M. "Alternatives to a Compensation Plan for Victims of Physical Violence." *Dickinson Law Review* 69 (1965): 391-405.

Culhane, James E. "California Enacts Legislation to Aid Victims of Criminal Violence." *Stanford Law Review* 43 (1965): 266-73.

Edelhertz, Herbert, and Geis, Gilbert. "California's New Crime Victim Compensation Statute." *San Diego Law Review* 11 (1974): 880-905.

Edelhertz, Herbert, et al. "Part I—Public Compensation of Victims of Crime: A Survey of the New York Experience." *Criminal Law Bulletin* 9 (1973): 5-47.

———. "Part II—Public Compensation of Victims of Crime: A Survey of the New York Experience." *Criminal Law Bulletin* 9 (1973): 101-23.

Ehrlich, Isaac. "The Deterrent Effect of Capital Punishment." *American Economic Review* 65 (June 1975): 397-417.

Eremko, James. "Compensation of Criminal Injuries in Saskatchewan." *University of Toronto Law Journal* 19 (1969): 263-76.

Ervine, W.C.H. "Compensation for Malicious Damage to Property." *New Law Journal* 123 (1973): 497-98.

Fahy, J.L. "The Administration of the Accident Compensation Act 1972." *Economic Bulletin.* Canterbury Chamber of Commerce, no. 592 (1975).

Garner, J.F. "The Criminal Injuries Compensation Board." *Public Law* (1967): 323-29.

Goldberg, Arthur J. "Preface." *Southern California Law Review* 43 (1970); 1-3.

Gross, Richard J. "Crime Victim Compensation in North Dakota: A Year of Trial and Error." *North Dakota Law Review* 53 (1976): 7-49.

Harris, Duane G. "Compensating Victims of Crime: Blunting the Blow." *Business Review.* Federal Reserve Bank of Philadelphia (June 1972): 14-20.

Harrison, David H. "Criminal Injuries Compensation in Britain." *American Bar Association Journal* 57 (1971): 476-81.

Harvard Law Review. "Recent Legislative Action." Volume 78 (1965): 1683-86.

Hochman, Harold, and Rodgers, James D. "Pareto Optimal Redistribution." *American Economic Review* 59 (September 1969): 542-47.

Jacob, Bruce R. "Reparation or Restitution by the Criminal Offender to his Victim." *Journal of Criminal Law, Criminology and Police Science* 61 (1970): 152-67.

Lambert, J.L. "Compensation Orders: A Review of Appellate Cases—I–II." *New Law Journal* 126 (1976): 47-48, 69-70.

Lamborn, LeRoy L. "Propriety of Governmental Compensation of Victims of Crime." *George Washington University Law Review* 41 (1973): 446-70.

———. "Remedies for the Victims of Crime." *Southern California Law Review* 43 (1970): 22-53.

———. "Toward a Victim Orientation in Criminal Theory." *Rutgers Law Review* 22 (1968): 733-68.

Laster, Richard E. "Criminal Restitution." *University of Richmond Law Review* 5 (1970): 71-98.

Linden, Allen M. "Victims of Crime and Tort Law." *Canadian Bar Journal* 12 (1969): 17–33.

Mansfield, Mike. "Justice for Victims of Crime." *Houston Law Review* 9 (1971): 75–80.

Miami Herald. 1975.

Miers, D.R. "Compensation for Victims of Crimes of Violence: The Northern Ireland Model." *Criminal Law Review* (1969): 576–86.

_____. "The Ontario Criminal Injuries Compensation Scheme." *University of Toronto Law Journal* 24 (Autumn 1974): 347–80.

_____. "Paying for Malicious Injuries Claims." *The Irish Jurist* 5 (1970): 50–69.

Mohler, Henry C. "Convict Labor Policies." *Journal of Criminal Law and Criminology* 15 (1925): 528–97.

Mueller, G.O.W. "Compensation for Victims of Crime." *Minnesota Law Review* 50 (1965): 213–21.

Newsweek. "The Doctors' New Dilemma." February 10, 1975.

New York Times. 1971–1975.

Note. "The Minnesota Crime Victims Reparations Act: A Preliminary Analysis." *William Mitchell Law Review* 2 (1976): 187–234.

Novack, Michael J. "Crime Victim Compensation: The New York Solution." *Albany Law Review* 35 (1971): 717–33.

Palmer, Goeffrey. "Compensation for Personal Injury: A Requiem for the Common Law in New Zealand." *American Journal of Comparative Law* 21 (1973): 1–44.

Pauly, Mark V. "Overinsurance and Public Provision of Insurance: The Role of Moral Hazard and Adverse Selection." *Quarterly Journal of Economics* 88 (February 1974): 44–62.

Plattner, Marc F. "The Rehabilitation of Punishment." *Public Interest* (No. 44, 1976): 104–414.

Prime, Terence. "Reparation from the Offender." *The Solicitors' Journal* 115 (November 19, 26, 1971): 859–61; 880–82.

Rawls, John. "Reply to Alexander and Musgrave." *Quarterly Journal of Economics* 88 (November 1974): 633–55.

Read, Bill. *Offender Restitution Programs in Georgia*. Atlanta: Georgia Department of Offender Rehabilitation, 1977.

Robinson, Michael, and la Villa, Gianluca. "English Criminal Courts and Compensation Orders." *Anglo-American Law Review* 4 (1975): 345–48.

Samuels, Alec. "Criminal Injuries Compensation Board." *Criminal Law Review* (1973): 418–31.

Shank, William. "Aid to Victims of Violent Crimes in California." *Southern California Law Review* 43 (1970): 85–92.

The Times (London). 1971–1977.

Tullock, Gordon. "The Charity of the Uncharitable." *Western Economic Journal* 9 (December 1971): 379–92.

Tullock, Gordon. "Does Punishment Deter Crime?" *The Public Interest*, no. 36 (Summer 1974): 103–11.

Vitali, Samuel A. "A Year's Experience with the Massachusetts Compensation of Victims of Violent Crime Law, 1968 to 1969." *Suffolk University Law Review* 4 (1970): 237–66.

Wall Street Journal. 1975, 1977.

Westling, W.T. "Some Aspects of the Judicial Determination of Compensation Payable to Victims of Crime." *Australian Law Journal* 48 (1974): 428–433.

Books

Becker, Gary S., and Landes, William M., eds. *Essays in the Economics of Crime and Punishment.* New York: National Bureau of Economic Research, 1974.

Borcherding, Thomas, ed. *Budgets and Bureaucrats: The Origins of Government Growth.* Durham: Duke University Press, 1977.

Buchanan, James M. *Cost and Choice.* Chicago: Markham Publishing Co., 1969.

_____. *The Limits of Liberty.* Chicago: University of Chicago Press, 1975.

_____. *Public Finance in Democratic Process.* Chapel Hill: University of North Carolina Press, 1967.

_____, and Tullock, Gordon. *The Calculus of Consent.* Ann Arbor: Ann Arbor Press, 1962.

Chappell, Duncan, and Wilson, Paul, eds. *The Australian Criminal Justice System.* Australia: Buttersworth, 1972.

Downs, Anthony. *Inside Bureaucracy.* Boston: Little, Brown and Co., 1967.

Drapkin, Israel, and Viano, Emilio, eds. *Victimology: A New Focus.* Lexington, Mass.: Lexington Books, 1974.

Edelhertz, Herbert, and Geis, Gilbert. *Public Compensation to Victims of Crime.* New York: Praeger Publishers, Inc., 1974.

Edwards, Chilperic. *The Hammurabi Code.* Port Washington, New York: Kennikat Press, 1971.

Garofalo, Raffaele. *Criminology.* Montclair, N.J.: Patterson Smith, 1958 (1905 edition).

Hibbert, Christopher. *The Roots of Evil.* New York: Funk & Wagnalls, 1968.

Knight, Frank H. *Risk, Uncertainty, and Profit.* Chicago: University of Chicago Press, 1971.

Leoni, Bruno. *Freedom and the Law.* Los Angeles: Nash Publishing, 1972.

Maine, Henry S. *Ancient Law.* 11th ed. London: John Murray, 1887.

Niskanen, William. *Bureaucracy and Representative Government.* Chicago: Aldine, 1971.

Oates, Wallace E. *Fiscal Federalism.* New York: Harcourt Brace Jovanovich, Inc., 1972.

Plate, Thomas. *Crime Pays!* New York: Simon and Schuster, 1975.

Powers, Edwin. *Crime and Punishment in Early Massachusetts, 1620–1692.* Boston: Beacon Press, 1966.

Rawls, John. *A Theory of Justice.* Cambridge: Harvard University Press, 1971.

Rottenberg, Simon, ed. *The Economics of Crime and Punishment.* Washington, D.C.: American Enterprise Institute, 1973.

Schafer, Stephen. *Restitution to Victims of Crime.* Chicago: Quadrangle Books, Inc., 1960.

_____. *The Victim and His Criminal.* New York: Random House, 1968.

Tullock, Gordon. *The Logic of the Law.* New York: Basic Books, 1971.

_____. *The Politics of Bureaucracy.* Washington, D.C.: Public Affairs Press, 1965.

_____. *The Social Dilemma.* Blacksburg, Va.: University Publications, 1974.

United States Code Annotated. St. Paul: West Publishing Co., 1975.

Von Mises, Ludwig. *Bureaucracy.* New Rochelle, N.Y.: Arlington House, 1969.

Wagner, Richard E. *The Public Economy.* Chicago: Markham Publishing Co., 1973.

Public Documents

Alaska. Violent Crimes Compensation Board. *Third Annual Report* (1976).

Hawaii. Criminal Injuries Compensation Commission. *Ninth Annual Report* (1976).

Maryland. Criminal Injuries Compensation Board. *Fifth Annual Report.* Baltimore, 1974.

_____. *Seventh Annual Report* (1976).

Minnesota. Crime Victims Reparations Board. *First Biennial Report* (1976).

New Jersey. Violent Crimes Compensation Board. *Annual Report: Calendar Year 1975.*

_____. *First Annual Report* (1973).

New York. Crime Victims Compensation Board. *1975 Annual Report* (1976).

_____. *Seventh Annual Report* (1974).

U.S., Administrative Office of the United States Courts. *1976 Semi-Annual Report of the Director.* Washington, D.C., 1976.

U.S., Federal Bureau of Investigation. *Crime in the United States.* Uniform Crime Reports, Washington, D.C., annual.

U.S., House, Committee on the Judiciary. *Crime Victim Compensation.* Hearings, 94th Cong., 1975 and 1976, serial no. 39.

_____. *Victims of Crime Act of 1977.* H.R. 7010, 95th Cong., 1st sess., 1977.

_____. *Victims of Crime Act of 1977.* 95th Cong., 1st sess., report no. 95-337.

U.S., Law Enforcement Assistance Administration and Bureau of the Census. *Trends in Expenditure and Employment Data for the Criminal Justice System: 1971–1975.* SD-EE no. 10, Washington, D.C., 1977.

U.S., National Criminal Justice Information and Statistics Service. *Criminal Victimization Surveys in Eight American Cities.* A National Crime Panel Survey, report no. SD–NCS–C–5. Washington, D.C., November 1976.

_____. *Criminal Victimization Surveys in 13 American Cities.* A National Crime Panel Survey, report no. SD–NCP–C–4. Washington, D.C., June 1975.

_____. *Criminal Victimization Surveys in the Nation's Five Largest Cities.* A National Crime Panel Survey, report no. SD–NCP–C–3. Washington, D.C., April 1975.

_____. *Criminal Victimization in the United States: A Comparison of 1974 and 1975 Findings.* A National Crime Panel Survey, report no. SD–NCP–N–5. Washington, D.C., February 1977.

_____. *The Nation's Jails.* Report no. SD–J–4. Washington, D.C., 1975.

_____. *Prisoners in State and Federal Institutions on December 31, 1971, 1972, 1973.* National Prisoner Statistics Bulletin no. SD–NPS–PSF–1. Washington, D.C., 1975.

_____. *Sourcebook of Criminal Justice Statistics–1973.* Edited by Michael J. Hindelang, et al. Washington, D.C., 1974.

_____. *Sourcebook of Criminal Justice Statistics–1975.* Edited by Michael J. Hindelang et al. Washington, D.C., 1976.

_____. *Sourcebook of Criminal Justice Statistics–1976.* Edited by Michael J. Hindelang et al. Washington, D.C., 1977.

_____. *Survey of Inmates of State Correctional Facilities–1974 Annual Report.* National Prisoner Statistics Special Report no. SD–NRS–SR–2. Washington, D.C., March 1976.

U.S., National Institute of Law Enforcement and Criminal Justice. *Exemplary Projects: Prosecution of Economic Crimes.* Washington, D.C., 1975.

U.S., Office of Management and Budget. *The Budget of the U.S. Government.* Washington, D.C., annual.

U.S., Senate. *Victims of Crime Act of 1973.* S. 300, 93rd Cong., 1st sess., 1973.

U.S., Senate, Committee on the Judiciary. *Hearings on S. 16, S. 33, S. 750, S. 1946, S. 2087, S. 2426, S. 2748, S. 2856, S. 2994, and S. 2995, Victims of Crime.* 92nd Cong., 1971 and 1972.

Washington. Department of Labor and Industries, Crime Victim Compensation Division. *First Report* (1976).

Index

Index

Accident, Compensation Act of 1972 (New Zealand), 10, 11
Accident Compensation Commission (New Zealand), 10
Advisory Committee on Victims of Crime, proposed federal, 40
AFDC, 25, 26
Agnew, Spiro, 29
Alaska, compensation program in, 32
Alfred, King, 8
American Bar Association, endorsement by, of governmental compensation program, 48
Amicus curiae, 13
Australia, 10; compensation schemes in, 16–17
Austria, 20

Bentham, Jeremy, 9, 65
Board of Appeals (Washington state), 33
Breton, Albert, 51, 52
Buchanan, James M., 66, 99
Bureaucracy, 3; model, Niskanen's, 51–54; theory of, 2, 45, 51
Bureaus, state: experience of, with fraud, 56–57; and incentives presented to lawyers, 57–58; and information dissemination, 58–59; natural expansion of, 56–60

California, compensation program in, 25–26
Canada, 20; compensation in, 17–19
Canadian Corrections Association, report issued by Legislative Committee of, 17–18
Carey, Hugh, 28
CBO. *See* Congressional Budget Office
Civil and criminal law, distinction between, 2, 3–4
Civil Evidence Act of 1968 (Great Britain), 14
Claims Advisory Board (Georgia), 38
Code of Hammurabi, 7
Collins, Arthur F., 26–27

Committee to Consider Compensation for Injuries through Crimes of Violence (Great Britain), 11
Common law, 8
Compensation for Victims of Crimes of Violence (1961, Great Britain), 11
"Compensation for Victims of Crimes of Violence" (1964, British white paper), 11
Congressional Budget Office (CBO), 46, 47, 55, 56
Conservative party (Great Britain), 11
Constitutional consideration, 66–69
Costs, potential, of national compensation program, 45–48
Court(s) of Claims: Illinois, 32–33; Ohio, 35
Crime(s): in American cities, 94–97; committed, number of, per sentenced prisoner, 92–93; growth of all categories of, 91–92; income from, 94, punishment for, 92, 93–94, 97
"Crime capitals," 94–96
Crimes Act of 1900 (Australia), 17
Crimes Compensation Commission (Florida), 36
Crimes Compensation Tribunal (Victoria, Australia), 16
Crimes Compensation Trust Fund (Florida), 36
Crime Victims Compensation Act of 1973 (Illinois), 32
Crime Victim(s) Compensation Board(s): Alberta, Canada, 19; Kentucky, 35; Michigan, 36; New York, 27, 28; Pennsylvania, 35–36
Crime Victim Compensation Bureau (Wisconsin), 35
Crime Victim Compensation Commission (Virgin Islands), 37
Crime Victims Compensation Division(s): Illinois, 33; Washington state, 33

119

About the Author

Roger Evert Meiners received the B.A. in economics from Washington State University, the M.A. in economics from the University of Arizona, the Ph.D. in economics from Virginia Polytechnic Institute, and the J.D. from the University of Miami School of Law. He was John M. Olin Fellow at the Law and Economics Center, University of Miami School of Law, from 1975 to 1978. He is currently assistant professor, Department of Management, College of Business, Texas A&M University. His most recent research interests include unemployment, patents, and corporation law.